Christmas

The Annual of Christmas Literature and Art

Christmas

Christmas

The Annual of Christmas Literature and Art

Volume Fifty-six

Augsburg Publishing House
Minneapolis, Minnesota

Table of Contents

In this volume . . .

Volume 56 of CHRISTMAS highlights the Christmas celebrations of Eastern Christianity. In the American cultural melting pot it has been Christmas traditions, more than anything else, that have preserved strong ties to the ethnic roots of many families.

Although the Christmas traditions of Western Christianity have influenced the national calendar and the American concept of Christmas, there is another Christmas tradition. This volume of CHRISTMAS highlights the customs, traditions, art, and music of some of the countries where Eastern Orthodox Christianity has dominated the culture. Donald Wisner's article on page 14 explains the difference between Eastern and Western Christianity.

The place of the icon in the piety of Christians in the Eastern world is acknowledged by the frontispiece, page 2, and the article on page 37.

The section, "Family Celebrations of Orthodox Christians," includes the customs of Greece, Russia, Romania, the Ukraine, and Armenia. If space had permitted, it could have included information on the customs of Syria and Serbia, as well. The lovely melodies of Ukrainian carols are printed in the music section.

The art illustrating the poem on page 49 is a style employed by Eastern rite religious artists of Ethiopia for many centuries. Tempera paint is applied to parchment.

The article on *The Nutcracker Suite* is included in this volume because it is by a Russian composer, living in the context of a country dominated, at that time, by Eastern Christianity.

In the theology of the Eastern church the manifestation of Christ, the Epiphany, which is symbolized by the visit of the Magi, has greater importance than the birth of Christ. The cover art, the poem on page 49, and the condensation of Henry Van Dyke's story highlight the visit of the Magi.

It is the prayer of the editors that your celebration of the birth of Christ be enriched by your neighbor's traditions in this holy season.

Editorial staff: Leonard Flachman, Karen Walhof, Jennifer Fast; Richard Hillert, music consultant.

The Christmas Story

According to St. Luke and St. Matthew

And it came to pass in those days that a decree went out from Caesar Augustus that all the world should be registered. This census first took place while Quirinius was governing Syria. So all went to be registered, everyone to his own city.

And Joseph also went up from Galilee, out of the city of Nazareth, into Judea, to the city of David, which is called Bethlehem, because he was of the house and lineage of David, to be registered with Mary, his betrothed wife, who was with child. So it was, that while they were there,

the days were completed for her to be delivered. And she brought forth her first-born son, and wrapped him in swaddling cloths, and laid him in a manger, because there was no room for them in the inn.

And there were in the same country shepherds living out in the fields, keeping watch over their flock by night. And behold, an angel of the Lord stood before them, and the glory of the Lord shone around them, and they were greatly afraid.

Then the angel said to them, "Do not be afraid, for behold, I bring you good tidings of great joy which will be to all people. For there is born to you this day in the city of David a Savior, who is Christ the Lord. And this will be the sign to you: You will find a babe wrapped in swaddling cloths, lying in a manger."

And suddenly there was with the angel a multitude of the heavenly host praising God and saying:

"Glory to God in the highest,
And on earth peace, good will toward men!"

So it was, when the angels had gone away from them into heaven, that the shepherds said to one another, "Let us now go to Bethlehem and see this thing that has come to pass, which the Lord has made known to us."

And they came with haste and found Mary and Joseph, and the babe lying in a manger. Now when they had seen him, they made widely known the saying which was told them concerning this child. And all who heard it marveled at those things which were told them by the shepherds. But Mary kept all these things and pondered them in her heart. Then the shepherds returned, glorifying and praising God for all the things that they had heard and seen, as it was told them.

Now after Jesus was born in Bethlehem of Judea in the days of Herod the king, behold, wise men from the East came to Jerusalem, saying, "Where is he who has been born King of the Jews? For we have seen his star in the East and have come to worship him."

When Herod the king heard these things, he was troubled, and all Jerusalem with him. And when he had gathered all the chief priests and scribes of the people together, he inquired of them where the Christ was to be born. So they said to him, "In Bethlehem of Judea, for thus it is written by the prophet:

'But you, Bethlehem, in the land
    of Judah,
Are not the least among the rulers
    of Judah;
For out of you shall come a Ruler
Who will shepherd my people Israel.'"

Then Herod, when he had secretly called the wise men, determined from them what time the star appeared. And he sent them to Bethlehem and said, "Go and search diligently for the young child, and when you have found him, bring back word to me, that I may come and worship him also."

When they heard the king, they departed; and behold, the star which they had seen in the East went before them, till it came and stood over where the young child was. When they saw the star, they rejoiced with exceedingly great joy. And when they had come into the house, they saw the young child with Mary his mother, and fell down and worshiped him. And when they had opened their treasures, they presented gifts to him: gold, frankincense, and myrrh. Then, being divinely warned in a dream that they should not return to Herod, they departed for their own country another way.

11

Now when they had departed, behold, an angel of the Lord appeared to Joseph in a dream, saying, "Arise, take the young child and his mother, flee to Egypt, and stay there until I bring you word; for Herod will seek the young child to destroy him."

When he arose, he took the young child and his mother by night and departed for Egypt, and was there until the death of Herod, that it might be fulfilled which was spoken by the Lord through the prophet, saying, "Out of Egypt I called my son."

But when Herod was dead, behold, an angel of the Lord appeared in a dream to Joseph in Egypt, saying, "Arise, take the young child and his mother, and go to the land of Israel, for those who sought the young child's life are dead."

Then he arose, took the young child and his mother, and came into the land of Israel.

13

Eastern Orthodox Christmas

DONALD W. WISNER

For the first 300 years after the birth of Jesus, the church did not celebrate Christmas. There was one major festival each year, and that was Easter. The anniversary of Christ's nativity was not recognized for two reasons: First, the early church wished to emphasize that salvation was dependent upon Christ's victory over death, which occurred at Easter; so, the death and resurrection were considered more important than Jesus' birth. Second, the first Christians did not want to be confused with the pagan custom of remembering birthdays.

Ironically, however, it was a pagan idea early in the third century that did influence the establishment of a second major festival time. Among the Egyptians, who were neighbors to the early Christians, the date January 6 was associated with the yearly awakening of the Nile River. January 6 was the winter solstice, the day in the calendar year when daylight is more prevalent than darkness. Christians borrowed the idea of water's renewing qualities and associated it with the water of Jesus' baptism and their own. A festival for Baptisms soon came into being.

The festival day was called Epiphany, from the Greek word meaning "manifestation" or "to make known." It marked Jesus' baptism when Jesus was introduced to the world as God's Son, who had come to be the light of the

world. It was natural, then, to associate the festival that focused on Jesus as light with the day when light was becoming more dominant in the physical world.

The Festival of Epiphany, or Baptism of Jesus, became a day when many Baptisms took place in the early church. New Christians were reborn in the waters of Baptism and shared in the life and light of Christ. As Christians, they were the ones chosen to make Christ known to their neighbors. They were to be the ones who would carry Christ as the light of the world and, therefore, be the agents of Epiphany.

A problem arose, however, concerning what actually took place at the baptism of Jesus, and it caused a serious misunderstanding among Christians in the early church. A group of people, the Gnostics, taught that before Jesus was baptized he was a man like any other man. On the occasion of his baptism, these folks taught, God the Father adopted Jesus; from that time onward Jesus might be called the Son of God. It took a council of the church meeting in the town of Nicaea to clarify this false teaching and reaffirm that Jesus was "eternally begotten of the Father" as we still confess today in the Nicene Creed.

Because of the confusion corrected by the Council of Nicaea, the early church fathers found it necessary to establish a separate day to observe Jesus' birth apart from his baptism. This festival focused on the virgin birth of Jesus and emphasized the divine nature of Immanuel, God with us. The Emperor Constantine chose the date

Photo: Greek Orthodox Church of the Ascension, Oakland, California.

December 25 for the celebration to be called the Nativity or as we know it, Christmas, meaning "Christ's Mass."

In order to describe Christmas practices in the Eastern Orthodox church, it is important to know who the Eastern Orthodox Christians are and how they came into being.

Before the year 257 A.D., there was one Christian church, but there were many powerful bishops within the church. Each bishop was in charge of a particular geographic area or city and was responsible for the congregations in that locale. The people used the language spoken in their particular area for worship. Since Christianity spread the entire length of the Mediterranean Sea and outward, an extremely wide variety of languages existed. Gradually, local customs also influenced the people's worship. Thus, Christians living in Greece differed drastically in their worship customs from Christians living in Rome even though they held to the same basic beliefs.

In time, however, even with many bishops, the bishop of Rome on the western end of the Mediterranean Sea and the bishop of Alexandria on the eastern end emerged as the most powerful and influential.

In the year 257, Bishop Stephen of Rome announced to the whole church that Jesus' statement quoted in Matthew's gospel (Matthew 16:18) was a clear indication that the foundation of the church's ministry should be in Rome. Stephen felt that since Jesus intended to found the church on Peter and that since Peter was considered to be the first bishop of Rome, all bishops of Rome were successors to Peter and the "rock" upon which the church was built. As a result, it was Bishop Stephen's intent that all other bishops and all other Christians should owe their allegiance to the bishop of Rome and look to him for spiritual direction.

Needless to say, the bishops and congregations in Eastern Christendom were not willing to accept this claim, and a split developed in the Christian church which still exists today and divides the church into Eastern and Western families. The churches in the West adopted Latin as the standard language for worship; the Eastern churches retained the local languages spoken in each area. The churches of the West recognized the bishop of Rome as Pope ("father"), and the churches of the East looked to the bishop of Constantinople as Primate ("primary bishop").

Western churches became known as the Roman Catholic church, and the Eastern churches called themselves Eastern Orthodox churches or churches of the Eastern rite. Eastern rite churches are like a tree with many branches, representing ethnic roots and local customs such as the Greek Orthodox Church, the Russian Orthodox Church, or the Serbian Orthodox Church. When considering Christmas practices among Eastern rite Christians, it is difficult to generalize. It is even more difficult to explore Christmas practices among Orthodox Christians living in the United States because ancient traditions have become Americanized.

To understand the Christmas practices of the Eastern rite Christians, we need to move beyond the appearance of customs, traditions, and worship practices to determine what the church emphasizes in its teachings. With that caution in mind, we explore Christmas practices in the Eastern Orthodox churches.

A Dialog with God

GEORGE MUEDEKING

To the worshiper from the Western world, participation in an Eastern Orthodox worship service is a strange and mystical experience.

The air is heavy with incense. The walls are hung with elaborate icons—abstract, stylized portraits of the saints and members of the holy family. Innumerable candles, with their flickering and subdued radiance, light the interior. These are regularly placed before detached icon stations by devout worshipers, who reverently kiss the icons. Busy and absorbed priests, deacons, and acolytes in bejeweled and resplendent robes move in an incense haze around the central segregated holy table. They ritually and frequently embrace each other and kiss the holy things of the altar. They disappear and reappear through doors cut in the iconostasis, a wall of banked icons separating the bema or sanctuary from the assembly of believers.

Worship takes the form of a two or three hour, continuously sustained dialog with God, offered with full throated, harmonized antiphonal chanting between priests, deacons, and choir. When the Creed, the Lord's Prayer, and the resurrection hymn are recited in song, the congregation also enters the dialog. Worshipers repeatedly cross themselves as they stand in reverent attention. No pews are found in the Slavonic-speaking churches. In the Greek-speaking churches of the U.S.A., however, worshipers are seated.

This is Orthodoxy, the original Christian church, which now embraces 200 million members. These worship services—liturgies judged to be masterpieces of religious literature—are conducted in the language of its varied nationalities. This means that although Orthodoxy reached the United States from Russia in the early 1800s, the American worshiper typically engages in a bilingual experience. The liturgy switches back and forth between English and the worshipers' native tongue. The original language may be Greek, Russian, Georgian, Ukrainian, Serbian, Romanian, Bulgarian, Syrian, Egyptian, Armenian, Ethiopian, or Malabar Indian, to name most of the Eastern constituent churches.

The Greek Orthodox Church in America, the largest of the American Orthodox denominations, celebrates the Epiphany festival on the same date as other European and American churches do—January 6. Russian and most slavic-speaking Orthodox churches, however, celebrate the festival on January 19. These churches still follow the Julian calendar (worked out by Julius Caesar), which is 13 days behind the Western calendar devised by Pope Gregory XIII in 1582. (Of course, it is January 6 to these slavic churches also—but that turns out to be January 19 to westerners.) All Orthodox churches celebrate Easter according to theJulian calendar; so the date for this latter festival also varies from our Western calendar.

Christmas in the Orthodox calendar is one of 12 Great Feasts. The date of December 25 for Christmas, the Festival of the Nativity, was borrowed from the Western Christian churches about 386 A.D. It became a celebration added to the traditional January 6 observance of Jesus' birthday. The liturgy for the days of Christmas in Orthodox churches, therefore, includes the story of the Wise Men, in contrast to Western Christian calendars where the same story is identified with the Epiphany festival on January 6.

While the familiar and homely details of the swaddling-clothed babe and the manger cave are not omitted, the focus for the nativity feast lies elsewhere. The prayer-hymns of the Christmas liturgy center on the paradoxical union of humanity and divinity in the person of Christ: "A young child, the pre-eternal God," the liturgist sings. "Older than ancient Adam," the Christ lies in his mother's arms; the Creator makes himself the created, says the Compline Service for Christmas Eve.

The December 25 date for the observing of the incarnation of Christ was never able to supplant wholly the original celebration on January 6, called Epiphany or Manifestation in Eastern Christianity. As Father Thomas Paris, priest of the Greek Orthodox Church of the Ascension in Oakland, California, concedes, "Here in the United States we have virtually copied the Christmas celebrations of Protestants and Roman Catholics, including their Sunday school pageants." But he adds, "If you want to join in our deeper understanding of the miracle that he whom the universe cannot contain was confined to a cave, then come to our Theophany Feast on January 6."

Theophany ("God-manifestation"), as the festival is called, has four emphases. The first time the world was granted the full revelation of the nature of God himself as "three-oneness" or "trinity" was at the baptism of Jesus. So God-manifestation (that is, Theophany or Epiphany,) is pri-

Father Thomas Paris reading the Theophany liturgy.

Eastern Christians do not observe an Advent season in the four weeks prior to Christmas as is typical of most Western Christians. Instead, a 40-day fast period begins on November 15 so that the faithful may prepare themselves for the power of God to be displayed at Christ's birth. The mood of this preparation period is one of anticipation during which Orthodox members abstain from excessive eating and drinking, including the "pre-Christmas" parties which are so prevalent in our American culture. There are no special home decorations such as lights, trees, and wreaths, although in some communities Orthodox Christians copy their neighbors.

Followers of Eastern rites call this period the Sundays after Pentecost, and they conduct worship services according to the normal liturgical patterns with two exceptions: On the second Sunday before Christmas, called the Sunday of the Holy Forefathers, the lessons and songs focus on the saints in the Old Testament, the prophets and foretellers of the coming Savior. The congregations sing of Noah, Samson, Barak, Josiah, Job, Samuel, David, Solomon, Elijah, and all the prophets, including Daniel who survived a night's stay in the lion's den. They sing also of holy women such as Deborah, Judith, Ruth, Esther, Rachel, and Sarah who were strong in the Lord. The Sunday of Holy Forefathers (and Mothers) is important because it links Jesus with the age-old story of God's power among people. The Sunday before Christmas is called the Geneology of Jesus, and on this day the direct ancestors of Jesus are recalled by reading the account in Matthew's gospel.

With the 40-day preparation period complete and the solid link established between Jesus' birth and the continuous actions of God throughout history, Eastern Orthodox Christians then are ready for the celebration of Jesus' nativity.

On the day before Christmas, a strict fast is maintained by all Orthodox Christians, and churches are opened for prayer and vigil from morning to night. In homes, straw is often placed on the floor under the dining room table to represent the manger straw upon which Jesus was born. The whole household stands ready for the birth of God's Son.

In many homes at the sighting of the first star in the evening sky (Bethlehem's Star), the fast is broken and family members share in a Christmas Eve meal of simple but traditional foods, before attending vesper services at church. In church on Christmas Eve a service of vigil is held during which the priest reads an ancient version of Isaiah's prophecy from Isaiah 9. "God is with us," echoes the text to a congregation that now stands with the prophets, martyrs, and saints of old eager for the birth of the Savior. Following the service, worshipers return to their homes where gifts might be exchanged, although traditionally gift-giving was done on St. Nicholas Day, December 26.

On Christmas Day, the Nativity of Our Lord Jesus Christ, Orthodox Christians gather for a mass that uses ancient hymns. In particular, one hymn is chanted five times during the service. This hymn with its opening sentence, "Thy nativity, O Christ our God, has shown the world the light of wisdom," serves to introduce the basic theme of the day: Jesus Christ is God made flesh and given to the whole world, and on this day all creation gives thanks for that gift.

Icons are an essential part of all Eastern Orthodox worship services and are prominent in homes and churches. Icons usually are paintings or sculptures used to assist worshipers in devotion and prayer. On Christmas Day, the icon usually portrays the manger scene and helps the congregation focus their attention on the people who were present at the birth of Jesus.

An icon used on Christmas would portray Mary and the child Jesus. Mary is called the *Theotokos,* the "one who brings God." Joseph traditionally is pictured in Eastern icons as an elderly, white-bearded figure because, according to legend, he was an elderly widower subjected to temptation by Satan to doubt the virgin birth. Satan, the Prince of Darkness, is at times present in the icon, although his garments are dark and drab in contrast to other bright colors used. The Eastern church emphasizes that the birth of Jesus was immediately for the whole world, so the Magi, the visitors from outside Israel, are included in the Christmas story and icons. In most Western churches the Magi do not usually appear in the manger scene until Epiphany because, according to the gospel accounts, the wise ones were not present for the birth of Jesus. Angels also are included in the icons because their purpose was to worship the newborn King and announce his coming to the shepherds. Sheep, cows, and goats often are included for they represent the entire creation, which rejoices at the birth of the Messiah. A Christmas icon captures the enormity and the simplicity of the nativity, both the high and the lowly, heaven and earth, all responding to Jesus' birth.

The period of time between the Nativity of Our Lord Jesus Christ, Christmas Day, and the Festival of the Epiphany on January 6 is a time of celebration. Eastern rite Christians do not kneel during worship in the period between Christmas and Epiphany. Worshipers stand for prayer as a gesture of rejoicing and thanksgiving.

Each day between Christmas and Epiphany (called the Days of Christmas) has a specific theme and focus. The second day of Christmas is dedicated to the virgin Mary for she is the one through whom the Savior has come. There also are days set aside to remember Stephen, the first martyr, and others who died confessing their faith. On the eighth day of Christmas, Eastern Orthodox Christians gather to recognize Jesus' circumcision and his receiving the name Jesus, which means "savior." This day is important because it demonstrates Jesus' fulfillment of the law and his identification with God's entire creation story. A five-day preparation time precedes the Festival of Epiphany on January 6. On these days the prayers and hymns focus on the significance of Jesus' baptism and, in particular, on the role played by John the Baptist.

Jesus' baptism in the Jordan River by John the Baptist is the first public appearance of Jesus (alone) to the world, and in this "epiphany" he makes himself known to the world as Messiah.

However, not only is the festival of Jesus' baptism an occasion for self-revelation, but Epiphany also takes on extreme importance for the Eastern churches because this event is an occasion for making the Holy Trinity known. The Father, Son, and Holy Spirit—the full Godhead—are announced and revealed on this occasion. Thus, Jesus' baptism with the Holy Spirit present over the waters of the Jordan is linked to the Book of Genesis account wherein the Holy Spirit also moved over the

The distribution of the water which has been blessed.

marily the celebration of Christ's baptism in the Jordan for Orthodox believers. "When thou, O Lord, wast baptized in Jordan, the worship of the Trinity was manifested," says the dismissal hymn for this festival. It goes on, "For the voice of the Father bore witness unto three, calling thee the beloved Son, and the Spirit in the form of a dove confirmed his word as sure and steadfast. O Christ our God, who hast appeared and enlightened the world, glory to thee."

Christ as the light that enlightens the world is the second emphasis of this festival. In earliest Christianity, the eve of the Epiphany was the time for hundreds of neophytes to stand at the water's edge, each with torch in hand, to be immersed and thus to take up membership in the kingdom of light. This festival, therefore, became known also as the Feast of Lights.

The liturgical forms for this Great Feast ponder an ineffable gospel story: The Christ who was without sin requested baptism for himself. The only responsible theological commentary would be that in submitting to baptism, Christ represented his believers in their need for cleansing from sin through this rite. So the Theophany liturgy speaks of the Christian's baptismal renewal in Christ's baptism as its third emphasis. It uses virtually the identical prayer in the final liturgical drama for this day, called The Great Blessing of the Waters, that is used at the font at the sacrament of Baptism. As the sinless Christ died for all sinners on the cross of Calvary, so in baptism the Christ who needs no baptism represents his people in the baptismal acquiring of new life. They become part of him as he submits to his Jordan immersion to "fulfill all righteousness."

When Christ descended into the baptismal water of the Jordan, he also "sanctified" all water and, hence, all nature. Just as all nature and the angelic orders were involved in humankind's fall into sin and the whole cosmos was disfigured, so by Christ's immersion all waters and all nature were renewed. He overcame "the dragons in the water," says the liturgy, picking up Psalm 74:13.

The liturgy for Theophany, therefore, carries

17

as its fourth emphasis and climactic action the Great Blessing of the Waters. A spacious silver urn is filled with water. The priest takes the "precious cross" from the altar and dips it three times into those waters, thereby symbolizing Christ's cleansing of all water and of all nature. The faithful draw near to be sprinkled from a basil branch dipped into the sanctified waters. They also take the water home to drink, to wash themselves, and to sprinkle over their homes and family.

The Orthodox church has created a cultus, which in architecture, symbolic ritual, and liturgical song-speech has preserved the worshiping church as "an island of heaven on earth," to use St. Paul's description of the Philippian church: "We are a colony of heaven" (Philippians 3:20).

The tour guide at Oakland's Ascension Church, for example, instructs visitors, "Now when we walk through these doors, we will be entering the kingdom of heaven. On the ceiling you will see the painting of the Christ observing us as he rules over all heaven and earth and surrounded by his apostles and martyrs. Immediately over the sanctuary at the front, you will see the painting of the Godbearer, the *Theotokos*, the virgin Mary. She is always pictured as cradling in her arm the Son of God. She takes her central place because she is the ladder by which God came down to humanity. But she never appears alone. For she saves no one for eternity and is not to be adored as though she were worthy in her own right. Her Son, not her, is Savior of the world," the guide carefully explains.

When one worships with Orthodox Christians one enters upon a rich world of history and dedication, preserved through liturgies that exult unchangedness century after century. The use of drama and of each of the senses in worship brings the "presentness" of Christ in the assembly of believers into vivid recognition. Often called "the candlelight kingdom" for its bountiful use of candles in worship, the church is self-conscious of its unbroken continuity, glorying in its existence as a creation of God.

The Great Blessing of the Waters in Theophany liturgy.

waters of creation. Once again, God's creative work is celebrated as continuous.

Foremost, therefore, among all the Eastern churches' activities on the Festival of Epiphany is the Great Blessing of the Waters.

Immediately after the Eucharist or Holy Communion, the priest and congregation chant special prayers and hymns over a large container of water. This container of water, decorated with candles and flowers, is the symbol of the beautiful world which God once created. Following the Great Blessing of the Waters, the congregation is invited to drink the water and remind themselves in this tangible way of their own link to creation by their Baptism. Not only are they reminded of Baptism, but, on this occasion, God's power also resides within them.

Following the worship service on the Festival of Epiphany, the priest takes the remaining water and visits the home of each member. He blesses their dwelling and accompanies the blessing with the Rite of Exorcism. As a result, Satan's power is vanquished and the power of God now reigns.

In the Eastern Orthodox church, the Festival of Epiphany lasts seven days, ending 40 days after Christmas Day. On February 2 the Meeting of Our Lord in the Temple is commemorated. On this day, the gospel account of Jesus' presentation to the aged Anna and Simeon in the temple is read. This day has as its focus the merging of the old covenant God made with Israel and the new covenant God presents in Christ. Now, not only Israel but all nations may know the salvation that God offers to sinful people.

Orthodox Christians have preserved the tradition of the Epiphany cake, and some churches and families of Western Christianity copy the custom. According to legend, centuries ago in 380 A.D., the greedy governor of Caesarea was accustomed to dipping his hands into the churches' monies whenever he felt the need for ready cash. Basil, the Bishop of Caesarea, proposed to his congregations that they offer the governor all their valuable jewelry, gold, and silver. On Epiphany that year, the governor attended Basil's church and was moved by the bishop's sermon, which focused on "rendering to God the things which are God's and to Caesar the things that are Caesar's." Upon hearing the sermon, the governor was moved to the point where he promised to stop stealing from the church and returned all the people's valuables to Basil. Basil did not know what to do with all the returned jewelry, so he baked cakes which contained the gold and silver and had the loaves distributed to the poor.

According to legend, a person who finds a valuable object in a piece of cake on Epiphany will have good fortune all year. In some churches today, a cake containing a ring is baked on Epiphany. The person who eats the piece of cake which contains the ring will receive good fortune and must furnish the cake the following year.

Christians in the Eastern churches have much to contribute to the rest of Christianity. We all could benefit from the simplicity of the Orthodox practice and its lack of commercialism. It might help us to remember that Christmas is not an antique event which took place in Bethlehem's stable but rather is a continuing occasion for the revealing of God's powerful promises in the whole world.

Russia

St. Nicholas, beloved friend of children and mysterious dispenser of gifts at Christmas throughout the world, has been the patron of Russia for centuries. However, in Russia it is *Baboushka* who is the bearer of gifts. The legend tells of old *Baboushka* ("grandmother") who is said to have misdirected the Wise Men when they inquired the way to Bethlehem. She repented the next day but since then is known to be roaming the world looking for the child Jesus. She tries to make amends by giving gifts to children.

On Christmas Eve, before the *kolydaki* ("carols") and the *badynak* ("burning log"), the Russian people celebrate their ritual Christmas Eve meal known as the "holy supper." The entire day is spent preparing the foods served at this family meal for which everyone is required to be at home. If any members have died or have to be away, an empty place is set for them. The shades are drawn and a single candle is lit in the center of the white tablecloth to signify the star of Bethlehem. As a symbol of love and peace, a wafer of bread imprinted with nativity scenes is served by the father to his wife and children before the meal begins.

When everyone is seated, 12 courses are eaten one by one in honor of the 12 apostles who proclaimed the gospel. The meal begins with a bitter taste of garlic (*chesnok*) and ends with sweets, such as bread with honey (*foochki*), to remind the family of the bitterness of the world before Christ came, bringing sweetness at his birth.

Greece

Christmas preparations in Greece begin on November 15 with a 40-day fast. Carols are sung on Christmas Eve, but the real celebration begins at dawn on December 25 with the Divine Liturgy. The family receives Holy Communion as the culmination for which the fast has prepared them.

At home the family continues the celebration with *yalopoúla* (turkey) or roast pig along with *Christopsomo*, ("Christ bread"), which is baked with a cross carved on the top of the dough.

For the people of Greece name days are cause for celebration, since Baptism is a reminder of spiritual birth. On Christmas Day special visits are paid to persons with the name of Chris, Christine, and Emmanuel. They receive gifts, and open houses in their honor may last the entire day.

Family gifts are exchanged on New Year's Eve to usher in the New Year on January 1, the feast of St. Basil, patron of Greece. St. Basil was an early father of the church who astonished the pagan world by giving up his wealth to help the poor when he became Christian. Because legend says he often baked bread with a coin inside for the poor, just before midnight the head of the family cuts and shares *Vasilópita* ("Basil's bread"). The first piece is for Christ, the second for his mother Mary, the third for St. Basil, the fourth for the oldest child, and so on down to the youngest. Whoever finds a coin in his or her piece hopes for special blessings in the New Year.

Armenia

Among the Eastern peoples, only the Armenians celebrate Christmas on January 18, which is Epiphany according to the old Julian calendar. After a day of fasting, villagers gather on Christmas Eve at the church and celebrate a service of Holy Communion. Upon returning home, the women in the family light up the house and provide a special dish of pilaf, a rice food. This symbolizes that the fast is over and the merrymaking can begin.

The children then scramble to the housetops, hang handkerchiefs over the roofs, and sing:

> Rejoice and be glad,
> Open your bag
> And fill our handkerchiefs.
> Halleluiah! Halleluiah!

The family and relatives in the house fill the hanging handkerchiefs with raisins and fried wheat, sometimes tying some coins into them as well.

The main meal on Christmas Eve is shredded chicken breast cooked with wheat, cinnamon, and olive oil. Young Armenian men try to win the heart of their special girl by presenting her with a tray of cakes, eggs, raisins, and sweetmeats.

On Christmas morning the children are again presented with treats from their parents and friends. Often, these treats are apples in which one or more coins have been stuck. It becomes a game among the children who have a good time seeing which one gets the most apples, as well as the most coins.

Ukraine

As the first star appears in the sky on Christmas Eve, Ukrainian children joyfully announce to their gathered family, "God's star shines!" This announcement signals the festivities to begin.

Growing of wheat is very important in the Ukraine, so Christmas is a time of thanksgiving and blessing for a good harvest. Symbolically, the father brings in a sheaf of wheat and places it upright in a corner of the room where supper will be served. The sheaf is called "Forefather," representing the forefathers of their country who first tilled the land.

The family gathers around the table dressed in their best embroidered shirts and blouses. The centerpiece on the table is a special bread called *kolach*, three round braided loaves topped with a candle, which is carefully placed on an embroidered tablecloth. A candle is lit in a window, also, to show welcome for a homeless stranger.

Before the customary meal of 12 meatless courses begins, a spoonful of each dish is placed in the feed of the animals out in the barn because they were the first to see the newborn Christ child.

Carols are sung after the meal. Perhaps the best known carol handed down to us from the Ukraine is the popular "Carol of the Bells." Then the family attends midnight mass together. Afterwards, they greet one another with the words, "*Khrystos razdayetsia*" ("Christ is born"), to which others respond, "*Slavite yoho*" ("Let us glorify him!"). Such is the spirit of the season.

22

Romania

Hoping for fresh snow on Christmas Eve, carolers group together from the villages in Romania to announce the glad tidings of Christ's birth. They move from house to house, singing and playing instruments for family and friends, and are given apples, dried fruits, and sweet cakes in return for their beautiful music. Coins are given also as donations to the parish church.

The carols sung by the Romanians and other Eastern rite countries, as well as many of the carols that have reached us in our day, were once pagan in origin. These *colinde* originally hailed the moon, stars, and sun. As these countries became Christianized, the carols gradually were transformed, calling all creation to honor the newborn king. It is generally believed that the feast of the nativity itself was established on December 25 in the fourth century to offset a pagan festival of the sun.

On Christmas Day, it is the children's turn to carol from house to house. Dressed warmly and in their best clothes, they go about singing and carrying the *steaua*, a great wooden star covered with decorative paper and hung with little jingle bells to announce their approach. Sometimes a picture of the nativity is set in the center of the star.

For 12 days, older children from the villages dress up and act out the *irozii*, scenes from the story of Christ's birth. They go from house to house in the days between Christmas and Epiphany presenting their drama and receiving coins in return.

A New Joy Descending

Ukrainian
versification, Gracia Grindal

Ukrainian
arr. Richard Hillert

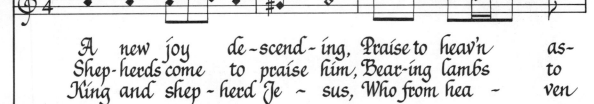

Majestically

mf

A new joy de-scend-ing, Praise to heav'n as-
Shep-herds come to praise him, Bear-ing lambs to
King and shep-herd Je ~ sus, Who from hea ~ ven

f

cend-ing, See the star shine bright as noon-day,
please him, Kneel-ing down, a ~ dore the Christ child,
sees us, Bless the mem ~ bers of this house ~ hold,

Custom and ritual, evolved over countless years, surround the singing of carols in the Ukraine. These are almost entirely of rural, agrarian origin; some practices date from remote antiquity. They also vary from region to region.

Christmas is celebrated in the Ukraine with the singing of special ritual songs called *koliadky*. A star-bearer walks with each group of carolers, carrying a symbol of the star of Bethlehem.

A New Joy Descending is traditionally the first in a series of songs offered by the carolers. It is sung before entering the house. After the carol, the leader of the group asks permission to enter the home, where additional carols will be sung.

The words of the carol evoke a pastoral scene suggesting the first Christmas, a characteristic shared with the nativity carols of many other lands. To Western ears there is a quality of refreshing originality in this majestic, slightly ornate melody.

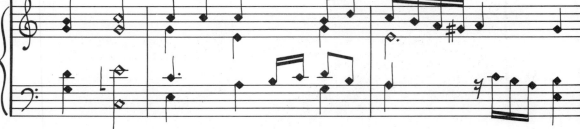

mp

Guid ~ ing shep ~ herds a new way.
Come to ran ~ som the ex ~ iled.
Keep them safe ~ ly in your fold.

Come, Tell the News

Ukrainian
versification, Gracia Grindal

Ukrainian
arr. Richard Hillert

Slowly

Come, tell the news to friend and to stran-ger, Je-sus is
Cher-u-bim sing with an-gels in cho-rus, Greet-ing the
O dear-est Je-sus, what can we give you, We have no

born in Beth-le-hem's man-ger, Ly-ing on hay, our
King who lies there be-fore us. Shep-herds have brought the
gold and we would not grieve you, But we can love you,

new lit-tle broth-er, Son of our God and Mar-y his moth-er.
best they can of-fer, Gifts for the child who came down to suf-fer.
life's dear-est trea-sure, You gave your life, a gift with-out mea-sure.

Carolers in the Ukraine are regarded as messengers of good news and are always welcomed guests. Upon entrance into the home they are invited to sing other carols. They are offered various treats as they are seated at the table, after which they continue singing and often dance in a ceremony of merriment that expresses good wishes to all.

The story of Christmas is recounted in many of the carols. It is pervaded with a sense of sharing and of giving, expecially in regard to the gift of the Christ child.

One such carol about the child's birth is **Come, Tell the News.** Its tune is that of a round dance; its text offers a simple version of the Christmas gospel.

25

Who Can Tell This Wonder

Ukrainian
versification, Gracia Grindal

Ukrainian
arr. Richard Hillert

Most traditions in the Ukraine do not accept the singing of folk carols in the churches. In some places only liturgical chants are used, while the *koliadky* are purposely confined to secular environments. But the biblically oriented carols of the people continue to be used in their celebration of this season, showing how important the message of Christmas is in their lives.

Just as traditions vary by region, so also there are numerous versions, both in words and music, of many of the carols. **Who Can Tell This Wonder** is an example of a carol that has appeared in many variant versions. The simple, plaintive melody and the imaginative folklike words reflect upon the mystery of the incarnation.

26

song   and she sings, "Je ~ sus,   son of   mine!"
song   and she sings, "Je ~ sus,   son of   mine!"

mine!"   Go to Stanza 2.   mine!"

The new year is a continuation of the Christmas-Epiphany cycle in the spiritual folk culture of the Ukraine. On New Year's Eve (*Malanka* or "Generous Eve") special songs (*shchedrivky*) are sung as part of the entertainment and merrymaking. They are usually sung by small children, but in the villages young men may sing them, going from house to house as they sing.

This cheerful festival inspired the most popular of all Ukrainian carol melodies, *Shchedryk*, which was written around 1913 by the composer Mykola D. Leontovych. The original choral version was first performed in Kiev in 1916.

The carol was later introduced to America in a slightly altered choral arrangement with entirely new words by Peter J. Wilhousky. This version, entitled "Carol of the Bells," acquired great popularity as a Christmas carol. It has been performed as such by virtually every professional and amateur choral group in the land.

The English translation that appears here for the first time reflects the traditional Ukrainian text. **Now We Are Here** is based on an ancient verse usually recited by small children at New Year's time. The musical setting offers the famous melody, with its simple four-note motif, in a version for unison voices and keyboard.

Now We Are Here

Mykola D. Leontovych
versification, Gracia Grindal

Mykola D. Leontovych
arr. Richard Hillert

Now we are here To wish you cheer For the next year To near and dear.

A swal·low flew Out of the blue, Home from the south Words in her mouth, Read·y to cheer

Those who would hear. She had good news From lamb·ing ewes. "Go, sir! she cheeped," Out to your sheep.

Go count the dams With bleat·ing lambs, Al·read·y born On this new morn. God bless your ewes

For this good news. You will have wealth, Love and good health, One dark-eyed wife

KANIUKA

In the Jordan River

Ukrainian
versification, Gracia Grindal

Ukrainian
arr. Richard Hillert

Calmly
p espr.

In the Jor-dan riv ~ er Where the tran ~ quil
Af~ter she has bathed him, Mar ~ y swad ~ dles
While he sleeps, the ox ~ en Keep their vig ~ il
An ~ gels hov-er near him Sing ~ ing praise to

wa ~ ters run, Stands our la ~ dy Mar ~ y
him in silk, Lays him in a man ~ ger
by his bed, See their warm breath steam ~ ing
Christ their Lord, And the Wise Men kneel down:

rit.

Bath ~ ing Christ, her new ~ born son.
Af ~ ter feed ~ ing him her milk.
In a ha ~ lo 'round his head.
All cre ~ a ~ tion is re ~ stored.

The words of **In the Jordan River** reflect the rituals celebrated at Epiphany (*Vodokhryshchi* or *Yordan*), the feast which ends the Christmas-New Year's Day winter cycle. In the spiritual culture of the people the eve of Epiphany is Second Holy Eve, on which rites similar to those of Christmas are repeated. On the day of Epiphany a solemn blessing is made using holy water; the house, the courtyard, and even the cattle are sprinkled with holy water by the head of the household.

The carol speaks of Mary as she bathes her newborn son, the Christ child, in the tranquil waters of the Jordan. The angels sing praises to their Lord and, as at the first Epiphany, the Wise Men kneel down to adore him.

The hauntingly beautiful melody of this carol is a reminder that the traditional music of the Ukraine contains a rich store of unexplored folk carols.

30

A Christmas Fantasy

The Nutcracker Suite by Pëtr Ilich Tchaikovsky

RICHARD HILLERT

It is all quite as fantastic as anything that could ever have happened "once upon a time." And, of course, like all entertainment fantasies, it is truly meant to be believed. Not for always, to be sure, but at least for the length of a good evening's diversion in the theater.

The fantastic pageantry of *The Nutcracker Suite* ballet has now attained the status of a perennial and indispensable Christmas favorite. The story, inconsequential in itself, is as old fashioned as any romantic fairy tale. Not a space thriller, it is rather intensely earthbound. Even when the heroine soars away hand in hand with Prince Nutcracker, they travel through the familiar, if enchanted, landscape of a snowy forest.

The popularity of *The Nutcracker* suggests that even romantic fairy tales have a place in the Christmas culture of our time. Written and first produced in Russia over 90 years ago, this fairy-tale ballet now takes its place within the hallowed array of Christmas ornaments that includes Handel's *Messiah*, Dickens' *A Christmas Carol*, and Menotti's *Amahl and the Night Visitors*. While perhaps not all these works represent the very highest artistic achievements of our culture, it is interesting to observe the fact of their popularity in the celebrating of Christmas. For many people one of the brightest of all Christmas decorations is *The Nutcracker Suite* by Pëtr Ilich Tchaikovsky (1840-1893).

In the world of music the selection of pieces known as *The Nutcracker Suite* has long been a popular concert favorite. Many listeners recall this piece as one that first provided for them a magical introduction to the wonders of symphonic music. Its appeal to the young even today is a very big compliment to Tchaikovsky and the enduring effectiveness of his art.

In the world of dance *The Nutcracker* can easily be counted the world's most popular ballet. It has brought to the ballet theater untold thousands of young and old who would not ordinarily attend ballet. It is the ballet for people who do not like ballet. The glow of its Christmas popularity is a tribute to the artists who have created its story, its music, and its choreographic productions.

Every major city in America now seems to have established its own *Nutcracker* tradition. It is conservatively estimated that several million people attend performances of it every year. The New York City Ballet maintains a four-week season with sold-out performances to over 100,000 spectators each year. In Chicago an annual season, also sold out well in advance, offers a lavish production and raises money for important charities. A few years ago the Warfield Theater in San Francisco presented *The Nutcracker* as a "Fantasy on Ice," starring the Olympic skating champions Dorothy Hamil and Robin Cousins. And many other cities and local companies, large and small, throughout the country present the ballet as an annual Christmas special.

There are several reasons for this popularity. In production *The Nutcracker* is extremely adaptable to the size of a dance company and its budget, great or small. It has been called the best friend a ballet company ever had. More than one regional group, not to mention established big city professional groups, have been rescued from deficit financing by its Pied Piper drawing power. It is profitable to produce because it does not require large forces of experienced and expensive dancers.

The cast requirements employ a large company of boys and girls and include miming roles that can easily be taken by nonprofessionals from the community. Many dancers have begun their professional careers with this ballet, not in starring roles but as one of the *Nutcracker* kids, perhaps as shiny toy soldiers or fluttering snowflakes or in the choir of angels.

But these reasons alone do not fully account for the popularity of this celebrated work. The general public, which ultimately supports the ballet with its enthusiastic attendance, has little concern for the requirements of dancing roles or even budgetary demands. Actually, there is no major ballet that requires less real dancing. *The Nutcracker* is as much a pageant as it is ballet. Its great appeal is as entertainment-with-music.

Bringing the story and the music together was the real genius of Tchaikovsky and his collaborators. How surprising that at its premiere in 1892 it was regarded as a hopeless failure!

The real origin of the ballet goes back to the early part of the 19th century when the German writer, Ernst Thedor Amadeus Hoffmann (1776-1822), wrote for his own pleasure a fanciful tale which he called *Der Nussknacker und Mausekönig* ("The Nutcracker and the Mouse King"). This extraordinarily imaginative children's story was first published in 1816. Like much of Hoffmann's writing it epitomizes certain aspects of literary Romanticism—the fascination with the unreal and the distortion and exaggeration of dream and illusion.

Hoffmann was also a gifted artist and an important musician of his time. He preferred above all to regard himself as a composer. A great admirer of Mozart, he even changed one of his middle names to Amadeus. He was prolific and quite original as a composer, but most of his music, including an important opera, *Undine*, has been neglected. He was, as well, a forceful, provocative, and influential critic who offered profound insights into the music of early Romanticism.

It is as a writer in the vein of German Romanticism that Hoffmann is remembered. The American Edgar Allan Poe and the Russian Feodor Dostoevsky were among those writers influenced by the way Hoffmann's prose combined the supernatural with the real and by his exploration of the sinister and demonic aspects of dreams and fairy tales.

Composers too were influenced by Hoffmann's literary work, notably Schumann and Wagner. The ballet *Coppelia* (1870) by the French composer Leo Delibes and the opera *Tales of Hoffmann* (produced in 1881) by Jacques Offenbach were based on his writings.

Another Frenchman, Alexander Dumas the elder, was so fascinated with Hoffmann's nutcracker tale that he made his own French adaptation, calling it *"Histoire d'un Casse-Noisette"* ("The Story of a Nutcracker"). Dumas' version eliminated some of the more grotesque elements and modified the action of the original story, but the basic plot remained about the same.

It was the Dumas version that was brought to the attention of Tchaikovsky and Marius Petipa (1819-1910), the brilliant Russian choreographer and ballet master. They had collaborated in 1889 on the ballet *The Sleeping Beauty*. When in early 1891 the St. Petersburg Opera invited Tchaikovsky to write another ballet, it was the subject of the nutcracker that was chosen. Petipa thought the story an excellent vehicle for ballet and eagerly worked out a libretto and planned the choreography with meticulously detailed instructions. Typical of the notes sent to Tchaikovsky are the following:

No. 1. Soft music. 64 bars.
No. 2. The tree is lit up. Sparkling music. 8 bars.
No. 3. Enter the children. Animated and joyous music. 24 bars.

And later:

Entry of the Mouse King—sharp angry music the sounds of which splits the ears . . . Clara throws her shoe—8 measures for a piercing scream and 6 for the whistling of the departing mice. The nutcracker is transformed into a prince—one or two chords?

At the end of his instructions, Petipa added with a gesture of self-confidence, "I wrote this; it is good."

Although many composers would have refused to conform to such rigorous restrictions, Tchaikovsky (with some reluctance at first) accepted the assignment. He was at the height of his creative powers during this period, although most of the popular works for which he is now remembered had already been written: the First Piano Concerto, the Violin Concerto, the *1812* Overture, *Romeo and Juliet, Swan Lake, The Sleeping Beauty*, and the first five of his six symphonies. He was about to embark upon the most extensive of his many conducting tours outside of Russia, to America.

Tchaikovsky began making sketches of the music for *The Nutcracker* during free periods in his travel time before setting sail for America in March 1891. In spite of the signs of appreciation and hospitality lavished upon him wherever he traveled, he began to feel his customary homesickness for his beloved Russia. In a letter to his brother he wrote:

Write all details [of events] to New York. Today, even more than yesterday, I feel the absolute impossibility of depicting in music the Sugar Plum Fairy.

That Tchaikovsky had attained the status of being Russia's foremost composer became evident as he reached America. In a letter to his nephew he wrote:

I am convinced that I am ten times more famous in America than in Europe. . . . Is it not curious?

He conducted concerts of his own music in New York for the opening of Carnegie Hall, in Baltimore, and in Philadelphia. By the end of May he returned exhausted from his triumphant American tour.

During a stop in Paris he had discovered a new instrument invented by Victor Mustel. It was the celesta, which he described as "something between a piano and a glockenspiel, with a heavenly tone." He immediately decided to have one sent to his home in Russia. Elaborate precautions were taken to make certain he would be the first composer to include the instrument in his orchestration. The special color of the celesta was used for the first time in a major orchestral score in the Dance of the Sugar Plum Fairy.

Music sketches for the ballet were completed in early July 1891. Tchaikovsky was not convinced he was the right composer to be doing this ballet and in one of his more pessimistic moments reflected his reservations in a note to his nephew: "It is far weaker than *The Sleeping Beauty*: the old fellow is getting worn out. . . ."

Before completing the orchestration, Tchaikovsky began work on a short opera, *Iolanthe*, which was to be his

tenth and last completed opera. It was to be featured on a double bill with the premiere of *The Nutcracker Suite*.

Upon returning from yet another of his relentless concert tours, Tchaikovsky hurriedly devised an arrangement of several numbers of the *Nutcracker* music for an orchestral concert that took place in St. Petersburg (now Leningrad) on March 7, 1891. Such was the genesis of the famous *Nutcracker Suite*.

The music was greeted with such tremendous applause that five of its movements had to be repeated immediately. This concert version of the music from the ballet has become one of Tchaikovsky's most performed orchestral pieces; its sheer popularity has served as first-class publicity for the ballet itself. *The Nutcracker Suite*, with its music taken directly from the ballet, is comprised of the following movements:

1. Overture
2. March
3. Dance of the Sugar Plum Fairy
4. Russian Dance
5. Arabian Dance
6. Chinese Dance
7. Dance of the Toy Flutes
8. Waltz of the Flowers

The charm, color, humor, and melodic appeal make this music a sure-fire winner wherever it is performed.

Audiences everywhere react enthusiastically to *The Nutcracker Suite* music, but the first performance of the ballet was far from successful. It was premiered at Christmastime on December 17, 1892, at the Maryinsky Theater in St. Petersburg. The scenario devised for the ballet by Petipa and his associate Lev Ivanov arranged Hoffmann's story, modified in the Dumas version, into two acts with three tableaux (scenes or settings):

Overture. This short orchestral introduction sets the scene of the action. It evokes a Mozartian atmosphere, reflecting Tchaikovsky's life-long admiration for his favorite composer, Mozart, to whom he paid musical tribute on several occasions.

Act I, tableau 1. A Christmas celebration is taking place at the cozy home of Judge and Frau Silberhaus in the city of Nuremberg, Bavaria. Their children, Fritz and Marie (named "Clara" in the Dumas version), are enjoying the festivities with great expectation. The highlight of the evening is the presentation of special gifts from Godfather Drosselmeyer. Marie's gift from the godfather is a nutcracker dressed in a flamboyant hussar's uniform. During the evening Fritz carelessly breaks the nutcracker's jaw, much to Marie's great distress.

When all is quiet after the party Marie slips out of her bed to see the Christmas gifts again. The room is suddenly invaded by an army of mice led by the Mouse King, an ugly, grotesque creature with seven heads and a crown for each head. Marie is startled as the toys become alive and go into action under the command of her beloved nutcracker. A ferocious battle follows, with the toy soldiers far outnumbered. Just as they are about to lose the battle, Marie in a fit of desperation throws her shoe at the Mouse King, driving them all away. (In Hoffmann's story the Mouse King is killed, of course!) Suddenly the nutcracker is transformed into a dashing young cavalier.

Act I, tableau 2. Prince Nutcracker now sails away through the Pine Forest with Marie. The landscape is filled with the flurry of sparkling snowflakes.

Act II, tableau 3. They arrive at the Magic Castle on Sugar Mountain in the Kingdom of Sweets. Here follows the Divertissment: Marie and the Prince are entertained by a series of colorful dances, a veritable Disneyland of stopping off places. They visit Candy Meadow, Gingerbread Valley, Honey Stream, and Confectionary Castle. There is no specific plot, just a series of representations. Hot chocolate is the Spanish Dance by a flamenco dancer in black and red, dancing with beautiful senoritas. Coffee is represented in the Arabian Dance, tea in the Chinese Dance. There is an episode from Hans Christian Andersen, The Old Woman Who Lived in a Shoe. The Russian Dance, the Dance of the Toy Flutes, and the Waltz of the Flowers are all part of the entertainment.

The second to the last dance is the *pas de deax* (the featured "dance for two" that is traditionally a part of classical ballet). One of its variations is the celesta piece, Dance of the Sugar Plum Fairy. At the close of the ballet there is a grand waltz finale and an apotheosis in which everyone proclaims Marie as the heroine and she and her Prince Nutcracker sail off into the sky as the dancers wave farewell—a magical ending.

The staging of the ballet finally brought together Hoffmann's fantastic tale and Tchaikovsky's vividly descriptive music. Premiering with the new opera *Iolanthe*, the work was not a theatrical success. Even though Tsar Alexander

Photo: Marie is crowned by the Nutcracker and Snow Queen at the end of Act I.

III himself attended and was "full of compliments," the critics all seemed to agree in their dislike of the production. The Christmas ballet, they wrote, was lacking in dramatic cohesion, and the dances were uninspired. Only the Waltz of the Snowflakes and the adagio of the Sugar Plum Fairy sequence were praised.

Tchaikovsky himself, although keenly disappointed with the cool reception, later admitted the ballet was "a little boring, despite the magnificence of the setting." The new ballet, together with the opera, fell into a period of obscurity. The opera, unlike the ballet, has not yet been successfully revived.

One of the reasons sometimes given for the early failure of *The Nutcracker* was that the choreographer Petipa had to withdraw because of illness, leaving details to his assistant, Lev Ivanov. But the production itself must have lacked luster and seemed to offend the sensitivities of some critics. One of them, Alexander Benois, an articulate and intelligent admirer of ballet, wrote, "The chief cause of my disappointment lies not in the music, but in the hideous production."

Criticism of the ballet should, perhaps, be tempered in the light of the restrictions imposed on the composer. One of Tchaikovsky's greatest gifts was his ability to express dramatic and profound human emotions in strong lyrical themes. These characteristics were out of place in *The Nutcracker*. Here the actions were emotionally inconsequential, the setting all tinsel and sweetly surrounded by the trappings of unreality. The situations were trivial and rather obviously devised for choreographic diversion. Nevertheless, Tchaikovsky treated the subject as well as and perhaps better than any other composer might have. The simplicity of his harmonies and the sometimes too obvious and rather prettified melodic material is somehow quite fitting to the story at hand. In retrospect it seems the production, rather than the music, was the cause of its initial failure.

Above all, *The Nutcracker* gave Tchaikovsky an opportunity to employ the greatest of his gifts, his virtuosity as a composer for the orchestra. His orchestration is full of invention and imagination. There are endless wonders in the varieties of orchestral color, in the sparkling and often surprising figurations and counterpoints.

Only one other major orchestral composition was to come from Tchaikovsky following *The Nutcracker*. His Sixth Symphony, titled *Pathetique*, was first performed on October 28, 1893. Tragically, the composer died only nine days later. His death came as a shock to all who knew him, and its circumstances, even according to the most recent and reliable findings, have never been conclusively determined. The pessimistic atmosphere that pervades his last symphony, which came to be regarded as a premonition of his own death, could not be farther removed from the vivacious and colorful pageantry of his *Nutcracker* ballet.

It is abundantly clear that the ballet has survived the misfortunes of its premiere. It was scarcely performed at all outside of Russia until a notable Sadler's Wells production in Britain in 1934. Then the San Francisco Ballet gave its American premiere with great success in 1944. And 10 years later George Balanchine, who had learned the work at the Imperial Ballet School in Russia, created a sensation with his production for the New York City Ballet. Balanchine's version was presented in a famous telecast in 1958, an entertainment event that was to create a nationwide demand for the ballet.

Because there have been by now so many different scenarios for the ballet, the original choreography has virtually disappeared. What truly endures is the music of Tchaikovsky.

It is the nature of the Hoffmann story itself that invites so many different interpretations. These have been limited seemingly only by the extent of human imagination. There have been abstract, plotless versions and others featuring spectacular acrobatics; still others have included various multimedia trickery and a chorus of Santa Clauses in the Waltz of the Snowflakes (Tchaikovsky suggested a boys' chorus here). Inevitably there have also been Freudian interpretations intended to probe the darker psychological recesses implicit in Hoffmann's original story. Balanchine, in fact, has insisted that his enormous success with "Nuts" (as the ballet is affectionately called backstage) can be attributed to his return to a scenario that is closer to the German Hoffmann than to the French Dumas. "For Christmas," he says, "German is better."

Through it all shines the music of Tchaikovsky, the Russian composer. He would certainly be pleased to know that generations of listeners continue to be enchanted by the magic spell he has cast over their celebration of Christmas in the form of *The Nutcracker Suite*.

Photo: The Waltz of the Snowflakes was praised by critics at the ballet's premiere.

The Nativity of Christ

Russian Nativity Icon

PHILLIP GUGEL

The Russian nativity icon vividly portrays the Christmas perspective of the Orthodox church. Through symbolism and teaching about God's incarnation (becoming human) the icon presents Christmas as a "feast of re-creation."

The word *icon* is a Greek word meaning "image" or "likeness." The nativity icon is done in an art style dating back to the sixth century Byzantine Empire. Orthodox iconography is a purely idealistic art form. Through the Byzantine style we see forms that are not meant to be realistic in nature, but abstractions that reveal theological concepts.

The virgin Mary and baby Jesus are found in the center of the icon because the birth of Christ is the main subject of the painting. Bound by swaddling cloths, the Christ child lies upon a coffin-like manger within a mountainside cave. Christ's birth brings spiritual light to illumine the darkness of sin, death, and hell as shown by the black cave. Mentioned by Justin Martyr, an early theologian, and in legend, the cave replaces the stable in Byzantine nativity scenes. The swaddling cloths, which resemble burial wrappings, allude to Christ's death. Christ is guarded by an ox and an ass, signifying the prophecy of Isaiah: "The ox knows its owner, and the ass its master's crib; but Israel does not know; my people do not understand."

Mary's figure is larger than the rest, a sign of her importance in Orthodox piety as the new Eve. Her reclining position emphasizes Jesus' human nature and the Orthodox concern that it not be thought of as illusory. The gold bed sets Mary apart, emphasizing her importance.

Also out of scale, the idealized mountain landscape visualizes Habakkuk's messianic prophecy: "God came from Teman, and the Holy One from Mount Paran." References to the mountain in the Orthodox Christmas liturgy signify creation's fulfillment and salvation. In certain Christmas hymns Mary is called the "holy mountain."

The upper half of the icon portrays angels glorifying God and announcing Jesus' birth to humankind. Their hands are veiled, symbolizing contact with the holy. They bend down to bring the good news of the Savior's birth to the shepherds, who represent the humble, and to the Wise Men, who represent the learned. Each of the Wise Men is of a different age, attesting to Orthodox belief that God reveals himself to persons without regard for age or worldly experience.

The shepherd located center right joyfully plays his pipe in response to the angel's message. He represents God's chosen people, the Jews, who have received direct word from God about the Messiah's birth. The merging of events occurring at different times in one painting, such as the visits of the shepherds and the magi, is known as "continuous narration," a technique that was used frequently by medieval artists.

Two midwives, in the lower right-hand corner of the painting, prepare the infant's bath. They illustrate the Orthodox teaching that Jesus was subject to humanity's bodily requirements and needed to be washed like any other child having been born of its mother.

Across from them, the devil, in the guise of an old, bent shepherd, tempts a pensive Joseph. The figure of Joseph is separated from those of Jesus and Mary, indicating that he was not the baby's father. According to Orthodox liturgical texts, his sad expression comes from the devil telling him that the virgin birth was impossible since it was contrary to nature's laws. Thus, the icon seeks to warn us about the heresy of denying the virgin birth. Mary, however, gazes compassionately at Joseph, an indication that the Orthodox tradition counsels compassion and tolerance toward those in doubt over this birth's mystery.

One final detail, the Tree of Jesse, located bottom center, represents the words of the prophet Isaiah: "A shoot shall sprout from the stump of Jesse, and from his roots a bud shall blossom. The spirit of the Lord shall rest upon him" (Isaiah 11:1-2).

The icon's gold background gives it a warm, inviting atmosphere. The red colors direct attention to the figure of Mary, who also is draped in red.

Most of the icon's figures appear in profile and are two-dimensional. Their flatness is somewhat relieved by the light and dark linear highlights added to their garments, giving a sense of drapery folding over their bodily contours. The triangular mountain landscape is treated in a similar way. The uninitiated tend to associate the flat appearance of icons with primitive art, although icons actually are painted according to a series of sophisticated rules. The icon painter is not concerned with self-expression, but rather with the expression of the church's holy tradition. To attain true status as an icon, the painting must be blessed by remaining on the church altar during a mass.

The spiritual purpose of the icon is reflected in the fact that icons never appear realistic and the conventional laws of perspective are not followed. Byzantine icons use an "inverted perspective." Unlike conventional Western painting, where everything disappears on the horizon as it appears to the naked eye, an icon is painted as if the vanishing point were within the person viewing the icon.

In Orthodox churches, an icon of the nativity decorates the "iconostasis," a screen with icons in front of the altar area. "The Nativity of Christ" engages us in contemplation of God who came among us to recreate his universe and his people.

Christmas Plates:
A Danish Tradition

LEONARD FLACHMAN

The addition of a Danish Christmas plate to a collection is an eagerly anticipated tradition in thousands of homes around the world. There are two legends regarding the origin of the Christmas plate and plate collecting.

For the 1888 Scandinavian Exhibition of Industry, Agriculture and Art, the Royal Copenhagen Porcelain Factory produced an advertising plate displaying the company insignia or trademark. The plates, with a crown over three wavy lines (representing the three waterways through Denmark), attracted much attention. And when the royal family expressed an interest in purchasing them, a sign was placed over the plates for the duration of the exhibition: "Sold to Her Royal Highness Crown Princess Louise of Denmark." This plate is said to be the first commercial collector's plate.

A second tradition has it that at Christmastime wealthy landowners and merchants gave their servants and employees gifts of candy, cake, and food on plates made of wood or metal. Eventually the employers be-

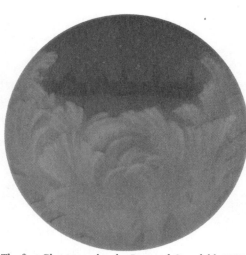

The first Christmas plate by Bing and Grøndahl, 1895.

came aware that their employees were collecting these plates and using them to decorate their plain living quarters. The plates given by one employer were compared to those given by another. Consequently, the employers began to seek out more decorative plates on which to make their Christmas presentations.

Harald Bing, of Bing & Grøndahl Porcelain Manufactory, saw the potential in such a custom and in 1895

produced the first Christmas plate. This plate marked a significant step in the manufacturing and marketing of porcelain plates in that it was the first plate to be dated, leaving the customer with the clear understanding that there would be another plate next year.

Ninety-one years later these two Danish porcelain factories, under wraps of great secrecy, are still designing an annual Christmas plate.

Work on the designs for the Christmas plates begins two years in advance of the date the plate appears on store shelves. The designer for Royal Copenhagen is given a general theme and at a specific time presents four or five art proposals to the design selection board.

Once the design has been chosen, a plaster model is made to show the relief affect on the plate.

Artist Kai Lange, who went to work for Royal Copenhagen at age 14, has designed 30 Christmas plates. His last design appears on the 1985 Christmas plate.

The work of a number of artists appear on the Bing & Grøndahl

The Bing and Grøndahl Christmas plates, 1896-1907.

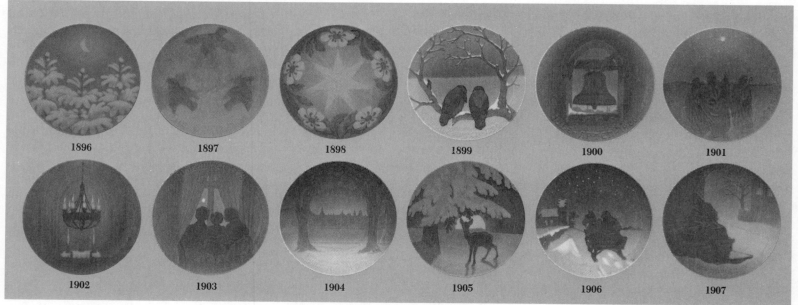

| 1896 | 1897 | 1898 | 1899 | 1900 | 1901 |
| 1902 | 1903 | 1904 | 1905 | 1906 | 1907 |

During the years 1908-1985 both the Bing and Grøndahl Porcelain Manufactory and the Royal Copenhagen Porcelain Factory have issued an annual Christmas plate. The plates by the two companies are shown side by side. The Bing and Grøndahl Christmas plates appear in the first and third columns; while the Royal Copenhagen Christmas plates appear in the second and fourth columns.

1908

1909

1910

1911

1912

1913

1914

1915

1916

1917

1918

1919

1920

1921

plates until 1963. The plate designs from 1963 to 1982 were done by Henry Thelander. The 1986 Christmas plates represent the work of two relatively new designers. The Bing & Grøndahl plate is designed by Edvard Jensen whose work first appeared on the 1983 plate. The 1986 Royal Copenhagen plate introduces designer Sven Vestergaard.

Neither company has a master plan or list of themes from which the designers must work. There are, however, certain popular themes that reoccur on the plates of both firms. Danish churches and places of national significance are the most popular themes. Family situations occur most often on the Bing & Grøndahl plates, while biblical themes and Danish churches are common Royal Copenhagen themes. Birds, animals, and nautical themes are also favorites of the designers.

Contemporary themes were employed in the design of two Bing & Grøndahl plates. In 1940 the German army put King Christian X under house arrest in the Sorgenfri castle. That castle appears on the 1944 plate. At the end of World War II, an oak cross was erected in downtown Copenhagen to honor the young Danish seamen who lost their lives. That cross is memorialized on the 1946 plate.

Because the early plates are not available to collectors who have begun collecting in more recent years, Bing & Grøndahl has issued a larger, 9-inch plate every five years since 1915 that presents a modified reproduction of an earlier design. The designs of the following years have been reproduced on the 9-inch plates: 1895, 1900, 1901, 1907, 1909, 1910, 1914, 1915, 1926, 1928, 1936, 1941, 1947, and 1950.

Royal Copenhagen issued two Christmas plates in 1911. One plate showing a snow-covered landscape with a lake, trees, and church was rejected and withdrawn from the market. About 120 plates, however, were sold.

The first Christmas plate issued by Royal Copenhagen in 1908, "Madonna and Child," was also issued in a German, *Weihnachten* version. The 1909 plate was issued in two additional versions, French (*Noel*) and Czech (*Vanoce*). In 1910 an English (*Christmas*) version was added. In 1941 the English version was dropped, whereas 1943 was the last year for the Czech version. Following production of the 1944 Christmas plates, the French and German language versions were discontinued.

For centuries Europeans were enamored with the high glaze pottery that trading companies brought back from China. The pottery was called porcelain because its eggshell color resembled the cowrie shell of the sea creature known as *porcella*. Thus, it became known as *porcellana*.

It took several hundred years, however, for European chemists and pottery manufacturers to unlock the secret of the Chinese porcelain. Today the ingredients of clay (kaolin), feldspar, and quartz are ground into a fine powder, mixed with a green dye and water, and formed into large, semi-firm paste pillows to await the production of the plates.

The master modeler carves the artist's design into a plaster model, creating the bas-relief effect that typ-

---

(top) Two years before a plate reaches the market, the artist begins work on the design. The design for each plate is approved by a committee before a plate is put into production.

(bottom) A master modeler creates a bas-relief model of the plate from which a bronze mold is cast.

1922

1930

1923

1931

1924

1932

1925

1933

1926

1934

1927

1935

1928

1936

1929

1937

ifies the Christmas plates. This model becomes the master for plaster of paris working molds.

The waiting green materials are mixed with water to produce a liquid porcelain, which is then poured into the plaster of paris molds. The plaster of paris quickly absorbs the water and a firm but fragile plate with a bas-relief design emerges. The green color of the porcelain enables those who remove the plates from the mold to determine if any of the white plaster of paris mold chipped off into the plate.

As soon as the plates have dried in the air, the green color disappears and the now cream-colored plates are moved by a slow moving conveyor through a kiln. As a result of this 950 degree firing, a hard, but still fragile, bisque plate appears.

The plates are now ready for the application of the paint, which combines cobalt oxide and gold. This water-base blue color is sprayed over

(top) After the initial bisque firing, the plates are ready for decoration.

(bottom) The color is a fine cobalt and gold powder added to water and sprayed on the plates. The porous porcelain bisquit absorbs the water, leaving a loose coat of blue powder.

1938
1939
1940
1941
1942
1943
1944
1945
1946
1947
1948
1949
1950
1951
1952
1953

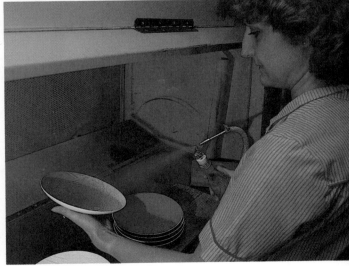

the surface of the plate. With a soft brush the artist removes the color in specific areas of the design. A second coat of the blue color is then sprayed on the bisque plate. With a shaped chamois "brush" the artist removes color from other specific areas of the design and the plate is sprayed lightly a third time. After firing, the blue color will be darkest where three layers of the blue color remain.

The blue plates, with very little of the design detail showing, are now ready for immersion into the glaze, a milky white quartz and feldspar liquid. The plates emerge looking much like the original cream-colored bisque plates.

While in the kiln for the second firing, the immense, 2500 degree heat causes the plate to shrink by a seventh of its size and to sag, so that the shape that emerges is not the same as what went into the kiln.

Following the 15-meter, 60-hour ride through the kiln, the plates are

(top) Using brushes and a soft cloth, the decorator carefully removes excess color to achieve the blue and white tones of the Christmas plate. The deeper the color coat, the darker the color will be.

(bottom) Each plate is signed by the decorator before glazing.

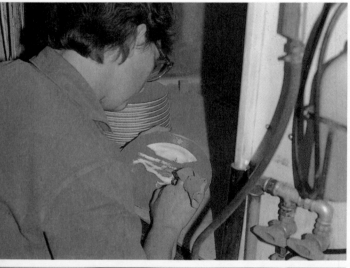

1954

1962

1955

1963

1956

1964

1957

1965

1958

1966

1959

1967

1960

1968

1961

1969

42

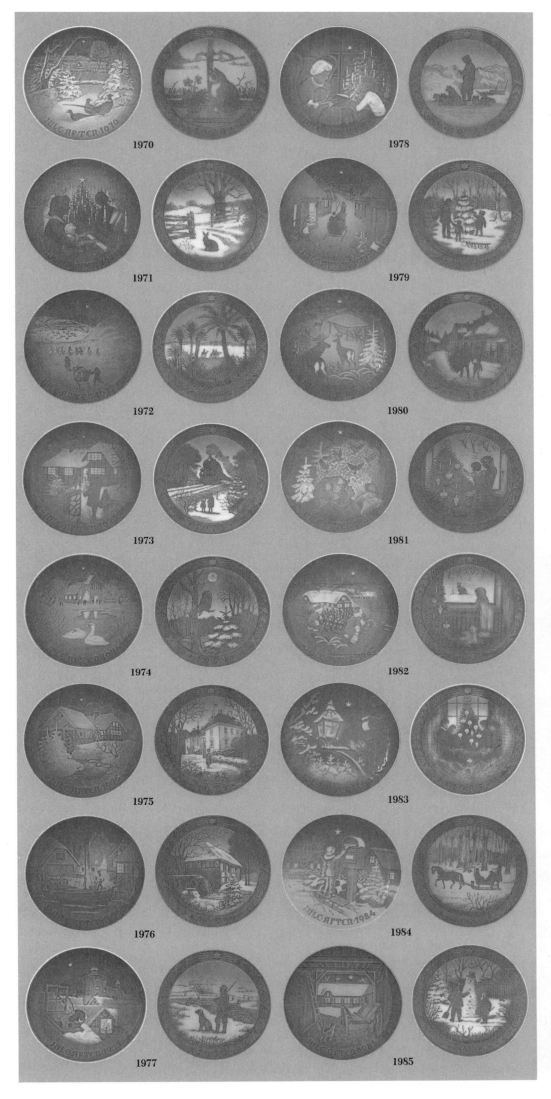

1970

1971

1972

1973

1974

1975

1976

1977

1978

1979

1980

1981

1982

1983

1984

1985

given two final touches. Any rough spots that appear on the bottom of the plate are ground off and the base is polished. Each plate is then inspected against a checklist of 30 possible imperfections. Such things as air bubbles in the glaze, a flaw in the mold, or an imperfection in the color will result in a plate being smashed.

Although the inspection is thorough, no two Christmas plates are identical. Because each plate is colored by hand the shades of blue cannot be standardized. Plates may appear in shops and stores in dark, medium, and light blue. Many collectors search carefully so that the tone of their new acquisition will match the rest of their collection.

Neither Christmas plate manufacturer will divulge the number of plates they produce each year; however, both have a ceremony each fall in which the original model is destroyed. Never again will that plate be produced.

(top) Before the final firing, the plates are immersed in a liquid glaze, turning them white. In the firing the glaze melts, bonding the color to the plate.

(bottom) A fired plate sitting on a bisque plate shows how much the firing changes the size, as well as the character, of the porcelain.

A Complete List of the Christmas Plates

Bing and Grøndahl

Year	Artist	Title
1895	F. A. Hallin	Behind the Frozen Window
1896	F. A. Hallin	New Moon Over Snow-covered Trees
1897	F. A. Hallin	Christmas Meal of the Sparrows
1898	Fanny Garde	Christmas Roses and Christmas Star
1899	Dahl Jensen	The Crows Enjoying Christmas
1900	Dahl Jensen	Churchbells Chiming in Christmas
1901	S. Sabra	The Three Wise Men from the East
1902	Dahl Jensen	Interior of a Gothic Church
1903	Margrethe Hyldahl	Happy Expectation of the Children
1904	Cathinka Olsen	View of Copenhagen from the "Frederiksberg" Hill
1905	Dahl Jensen	Anxiety of the Coming Christmas Night
1906	Dahl Jensen	Sledging for Church on Christmas Eve
1907	E. Plockross	The Little Match-girl
1908	Povl Jørgensen	St. Petri Church of Copenhagen
1909	Aarestrup	Happiness Over the "Yuletree"
1910	C. Ersgaard	The Old Organist
1911	H. Moltke	First It Was Sung by the Angels to the Shepherds in the Field
1912	Einar Hansen	Going to Church on Christmas Eve
1913	Th. Larsen	Bringing Home the "Yuletree"
1914	Th. Larsen	The Royal Castle of Amalienborg, Copenhagen
1915	Dahl Jensen	The Chain-dog Getting a Double Meal on Christmas Eve
1916	J. Bloch Jørgensen	Christmas Prayer of the Sparrows
1917	Achton Friis	Arrival of the Christmas Boat
1918	Achton Friis	The Fishing Boat Returning Home for Christmas
1919	Achton Friis	Outside the Lighted Window
1920	Achton Friis	Hare in the Snow
1921	Achton Friis	Pigeons in the Castle Court
1922	Achton Friis	Star of Bethlehem
1923	Achton Friis	The Royal Hunting Castle, "The Ermitage"
1924	Achton Friis	Light-house in Danish Waters
1925	Achton Friis	The Child's Christmas
1926	Achton Friis	Churchgoers on Christmas Day
1927	Achton Friis	Skating Couple
1928	Achton Friis	Eskimos Looking at the Church of Their Little Village in Greenland
1929	Achton Friis	Fox Outside Farm on Christmas Eve
1930	H. Flügenring	The "Yuletree" of the Town Hall Square of Copenhagen
1931	Achton Friis	Arrival of the Christmas Train
1932	H. Flügenring	Life-boat at Work
1933	H. Flügenring	The Korsør-Nyborg Ferry
1934	Immanuel Tjerne	Churchbell in Tower
1935	Ove Larsen	The "Lillebelt" Bridge Connecting Funen with Jutland
1936	Ove Larsen	Royal Guard Outside Amalienborg Castle in Copenhagen
1937	Ove Larsen	Arrival of Christmas Guests
1938	Immanuel Tjerne	Lighting the Candles
1939	Immanuel Tjerne	Ole-Lockeye, the Sandman
1940	Ove Larsen	Delivering Christmas Letters
1941	Ove Larsen	Horses Enjoying Christmas Meal in Stable
1942	Ove Larsen	Danish Farm on Christmas Night
1943	Ove Larsen	The Ribe Cathedral
1944	Ove Larsen	The "Sorgenfri" Castle
1945	Ove Larsen	The Old Water-mill
1946	Margrethe Hyldahl	Commemoration Cross in Honor of Danish Sailors Who Lost Their Lives During World War II
1947	Margrethe Hyldahl	The Dybbøl Mill
1948	Margrethe Hyldahl	"Watchman," Sculpture of Town Hall of Copenhagen
1949	Margrethe Hyldahl	"Landsoldaten," Danish Soldier from the Nineteenth Century
1950	Margrethe Hyldahl	Kronborg Castle at Elsinore
1951	Margrethe Hyldahl	"Jens Bang" New Passenger Boat Running Between Copenhagen and Aalborg
1952	Børge Pramvig	Old Copenhagen Canals at Wintertime with the "Thorvaldsen Museum" in the Background
1953	Kjeld Bonfils	Boat of His Majesty the King of Denmark in Greenland Waters
1954	Børge Pramvig	Birthplace of Hans Christian Andersen
1955	Kjeld Bonfils	The "Kalundborg Church"
1956	Kjeld Bonfils	Christmas in Copenhagen
1957	Kjeld Bonfils	Christmas Candles
1958	Kjeld Bonfils	Santa Claus Coming
1959	Kjeld Bonfils	Christmas Eve
1960	Kjeld Bonfils	Danish Village Church
1961	Kjeld Bonfils	Winter Harmony
1962	Kjeld Bonfils	Winter Night
1963	Henry Thelander	The Christmas Elf
1964	Henry Thelander	The Fir Tree and the Hare
1965	Henry Thelander	Bringing Home the Christmas Tree
1966	Henry Thelander	Home for Christmas
1967	Henry Thelander	Sharing the Joy of Christmas
1968	Henry Thelander	Christmas in Church
1969	Henry Thelander	Arrival of Christmas Guests
1970	Henry Thelander	Pheasants in the Snow at Christmas
1971	Henry Thelander	Christmas at Home
1972	Henry Thelander	Christmas in Greenland
1973	Henry Thelander	Country Christmas
1974	Henry Thelander	Christmas in the Village
1975	Henry Thelander	Christmas at the Old Water Mill
1976	Henry Thelander	Christmas Welcome
1977	Henry Thelander	Copenhagen Christmas
1978	Henry Thelander	A Christmas Tale
1979	Henry Thelander	White Christmas
1980	Henry Thelander	Christmas in the Woods
1981	Henry Thelander	Christmas Peace
1982	Henry Thelander	The Christmas Tree
1983	Edvard Jensen	Christmas in the Old Town
1984	Edvard Jensen	The Christmas Letter
1985	Edvard Jensen	Christmas Eve at the Farmhouse

Royal Copenhagen

Year	Artist	Title
1908	Chr. Thomsen	Madonna and Child
1909	St. Ussing	Danish Landscape
1910	Chr. Thomsen	The Magi
1911	Oluf Jensen	Danish Landscape
1912	Chr. Thomsen	Elderly Couple by the Christmas Tree
1913	A. Boesen	Spire of the Frederik Church, Copenhagen
1914	A. Boesen	Sparrows in Tree at Church of the Holy Spirit, Copenhagen
1915	A. Krog	Danish Landscape
1916	R. Bøcher	The Shepherds in the Field on Christmas Night
1917	Oluf Jensen	The Tower of Our Saviour's Church, Copenhagen
1918	Oluf Jensen	The Shepherds
1919	Oluf Jensen	In the Park
1920	G. Rode	Mary with the Child Jesus
1921	Oluf Jensen	The Marketplace in Aabenraa
1922	Mrs. Selschou-Olsen	Three Singing Angels
1923	Oluf Jensen	Danish Landscape
1924	Benjamin Olsen	The Christmas Star Over the Sea
1925	Oluf Jensen	Street Scene from Christianshavn, Copenhagen
1926	R. Bøcher	View of Christianshavn Canal, Copenhagen
1927	Benjamin Olsen	The Ship's Boy at the Tiller Christmas Night
1928	G. Rode	The Vicar Family on the Way to Church
1929	Oluf Jensen	The Grundtvig Church, Copenhagen
1930	Benjamin Olsen	Fishing-boats on the Way to the Harbor
1931	G. Rode	Mother and Child
1932	Oluf Jensen	Frederiksberg Gardens with Statue of Frederick VI
1933	Benjamin Olsen	The Ferry and the Great Belt
1934	Oluf Jensen	The Hermitage Castle
1935	Benjamin Olsen	Fishing-boat off Kronborg Castle
1936	R. Bøcher	Roskilde Cathedral
1937	Nils Thorsson	Christmas Scene in the Main Street, Copenhagen
1938	Herne Nielsen	The Round Church in Østerlars on Bornholm
1939	S. V. Nic. Nielsen	Expeditionary Ship in the Pack-ice of Greenland
1940	Kai Lange	The Good Shepherd
1941	Th. Kjølner	Danish Village Church
1942	Nils Thorsson	Bell-tower of Old Church in Jutland
1943	Nils Thorsson	The Flight of the Holy Family to Egypt
1944	Viggo Olsen	Typical Danish Winter Scene
1945	R. Bøcher	A Peaceful Motif
1946	Nils Thorsson	Zealand Village Church
1947	Kai Lange	The Good Shepherd
1948	Th. Kjølner	Nødebo Church at Christmas-time
1949	Hans H. Hansen	Our Lady's Cathedral, Copenhagen
1950	Viggo Olsen	Boeslunde Church, Zealand
1951	R. Bøcher	Christmas Angel
1952	Kai Lange	Christmas in the Forest
1953	Th. Kjølner	Frederiksborg Castle
1954	Kai Lange	Amalienborg Palace, Copenhagen
1955	Kai Lange	Fanø Girl
1956	Kai Lange	Rosenborg Castle, Copenhagen
1957	Hans H. Hansen	The Good Shepherd
1958	Hans H. Hansen	Sunshine Over Greenland
1959	Hans H. Hansen	Christmas Night
1960	Hans H. Hansen	The Stag
1961	Kai Lange	The Training Ship "Danmark"
1962	Kai Lange	The Little Mermaid
1963	Kai Lange	Højsager Mill
1964	Kai Lange	Fetching the Christmas Tree
1965	Kai Lange	Little Skaters
1966	Kai Lange	Blackbird at Christmas Time
1967	Kai Lange	The Royal Oak
1968	Kai Lange	The Last Umiak
1969	Kai Lange	The Old Farmyard
1970	Kai Lange	The Christmas Rose and Cat
1971	Kai Lange	Hare in Winter
1972	Kai Lange	In the Desert
1973	Kai Lange	Going Home for Christmas
1974	Kai Lange	Winter Twilight
1975	Kai Lange	Marselisborg Palace
1976	Kai Lange	Vibaek Mill
1977	Kai Lange	Immervad Bridge
1978	Kai Lange	Greenland Scenery
1979	Kai Lange	Choosing a Christmas Tree
1980	Kai Lange	Bringing Home the Christmas Tree
1981	Kai Lange	Admiring the Christmas Tree
1982	Kai Lange	Waiting for Christmas
1983	Kai Lange	Merry Christmas
1984	Kai Lange	Jingle Bells
1985	Kai Lange	The Snowman

The Other Wise Man

HENRY VAN DYKE

CONDENSED BY ARTHUR YEAGY

You know the story of the three Wise Men of the East, and how they traveled from far away to offer their gifts at the manger cradle in Bethlehem. But have you ever heard the story of the other Wise Man, who also saw the star in its rising and set out to follow it, yet did not arrive with his brethren in the presence of the young child Jesus?

Hear now the tale of the great desire of this fourth pilgrim, and how it was denied, yet accomplished in the denial; of his many wanderings and the trials of his soul; of the long way of his seeking and the strange way of his finding the one whom he sought.

Artaban lived in the city of Ecbatana among the mountains of Persia in the days when Augustus Caesar was master of many kings and Herod ruled in Jerusalem.

The location of Artaban's house was such that he could view with ease the beauty and splendor of the city he loved. Close by was a fair garden, a tangle of flowers and fruit trees, well watered, rich in fragrance and color.

Artaban was a tall, dark man, about 40, with brilliant eyes, and firm lines around his fine, thin lips. His appearance was that of a dreamer and also of a soldier, a man of sensitive feeling but inflexible will. He was clad in the dress of the ancient priesthood of the Magi.

Artaban held council with eight of his friends in an upper chamber of his house. The nine men varied widely in age, but were alike in the rich dress of Parthian nobles. They were followers of Zoroaster and worshiped as they shared in a chant, enlivened with music and a fire ritual.

Artaban spoke to his friends of the rekindling of their faith in the God of purity and of the many books that helped them untangle the threads of the mystery of life. He told them of the prospects of new light and truth, that there were many stars still beyond their horizon. The men spoke of the wisdom of the Magi and asked if any light could ever come which would forever dispel the darkness, the conflict they knew so well.

After some minutes passed Artaban drew from his tunic two small rolls of fine parchment. He unfolded them carefully and read the prophecy: "There shall come a star out of Jacob, and a scepter shall arise out of Israel." Some of the men were skeptical, recalling Israel as a scattered, captive people.

But Artaban continued. He and his three friends, Caspar, Melchior, and Balthasar, had searched the ancient writings and had studied the stars. A new star had been seen. When the star shone again they would set out for Jerusalem to worship the promised one who would be born King of Israel.

"We look for the star this night," Artaban said. "My three brothers are watching by the temple of the Seven Spheres at Borsippa in Babylonia, and I am watching here. When the star shines, they will wait for me ten days at the temple, and we will go on together. I believe the sign will come. I am ready for the journey. I have sold my possessions and bought these three jewels—a sapphire, a ruby, and a pearl—to carry as my gift to the King."

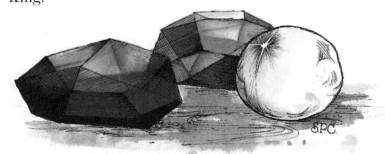

Artaban brought out the three gems from his inner garment—one blue, one redder than a ray of sunrise, and one as pure as the peak of a snow mountain at twilight.

His friends told him his dreams were vain; all had reasons why they could not share the journey with him. Only Agabus, the oldest and most loved, understood and gave words to lift the spirit of Artaban: "It is better to follow even the shadow of the best than to remain content with the worst. And those who would see wonderful things must often be ready to travel alone."

Artaban was left in solitude. He gathered the gems, watched the flame that flickered on the altar. As it sank he watched the western horizon. What began as a steel-blue spark rose through rays of saffron and orange to a point of white radiance!

Artaban bowed his head. "It is the sign," he said. "The King is coming, and I will go to meet him."

Vasda, the swiftest of Artaban's horses, had been prepared for the journey. She pawed impatiently, as if she sensed the eagerness of her master's purpose. Before the morning mists rose, the other Wise Man was in the saddle, riding swiftly into the west. Horse and rider were as comrades as the long journey began.

Artaban had counted carefully how far each day's journey would have to take him if he were to meet his three companions at Borsippa before they set out for Jerusalem. There were swift hoofbeats along the road as he crossed level plains, passed through forests, made his way through desolate passes, forded rivers, traversed fertile valleys. Each night's sleep was sweet; each morning his mount, rested, was ready for the toil of the day. They traveled late into each evening and went on again each morning before sunrise.

He pressed on and arrived at nightfall on the tenth day beneath the shattered walk of Babylon. Vasda was almost spent, but it was yet three hours journey to the Temple of the Seven Spheres; he must be there before midnight if he would find his comrades waiting.

Artaban rode steadily on. Vasda slackened her pace as they came to a shadowed place. She sensed some danger or difficulty. She carried her head low and at last stood stock-still, quivering in every muscle.

Artaban dismounted. The starlight revealed the form of a man lying in the road. Poorly dressed, of haggard face, he seemed to the traveler but a body ready for burial in the manner of the desert. But as Artaban turned, a faint ghostly sigh came from the man's lips, and bony fingers gripped the hem of the Magian's robe and held him fast. His heart leaped to his throat, not with fear, but with a dumb resentment at this blind delay.

How could he delay a minute to help the dying stranger? Should he linger an hour he could not reach Borsippa at the appointed time. His friends would think he had given up the journey. They would go without him.

But if he went on now the man would surely die. If he stayed, life might be restored. The struggle surged within him. Should he risk the great reward of his faith? Should he halt for a deed of life-giving charity? "God of truth and purity," he prayed, "direct me in the holy path, the way of wisdom which only thou knowest."

He turned to the sick man, carried him to the foot of a palm tree, brought water from a small canal nearby, and moistened the sufferer's brow and mouth. A potent remedy he carried was poured between the colorless lips. Hour after hour he labored; at last the man's strength returned; he sat up and looked about him.

The man, a Jew, said, "Who are you? Why did you trouble yourself to bring me back to life?"

"I am Artaban the Magian. I am going to Jerusalem to search for him who is to be born King of the Jews. But I can wait no longer, for the caravan that waits for me may go on without me. I leave you bread and water, and healing herbs."

The Jew raised a trembling hand in blessing. "I have nothing to give you in return, only this: I can tell you that the Messiah shall be born not in Jerusalem, but in Bethlehem, for so the prophets say. May the Lord bring you safely to that place, because you had pity for a sick man."

Artaban mounted and rode on in haste. As the sun rose he came to the Temple of the Seven Spheres. He paused, dismounted, climbed to a hilltop, looked toward the west. He glanced down, saw a papyrus message among some broken bricks. He read: "We can wait no longer. We go to find the King. Follow us across the desert."

Artaban sat in despair. "How can I cross the desert with no food and with a spent horse? I must go into Babylon, sell my sapphire, buy camels and provisions for the journey. I may never overtake my friends. Dear God, shall I lose the sight of the King because I tarried to show mercy?"

The journey across the desert was long and cruel. Artaban, high upon the back of his camel, rocked steadily onward like a ship over the waves. The desert was a land of death; of stony wastes; dark hedges of rock; shifting treacherous hills of sand; fierce heat by day; piercing cold by night. Jackals prowled and barked; from the lion came a hollow roar. Through heat and cold the Magian moved steadily on.

In due time we see Artaban in Damascus, then along the ridges of Mount Hermon, in the Valley of the Jordan, by Galilee's blue waters, among the highlands of Judah. He moved steadily on until he arrived at Bethlehem.

It was only three days after the three Wise Men had found Mary and Joseph and the young child, Jesus, in the place and left their gifts of gold and frankincense and myrrh.

Artaban, weary but full of hope, bearing his ruby and pearl to offer to the King, said, "Now at last I shall surely find him!"

But the streets of Bethlehem were deserted. Perhaps the men had gone to the pastures to tend their sheep. From the open door of a cottage he heard the voice of a young mother singing to her baby. She met him and told of the strangers from the East who said they had been guided by a star to the place where Joseph of Nazareth and his wife and newborn child lodged.

"But the travelers left suddenly, and Mary and Joseph and the child fled secretly by night," she continued. "We fear greatly that evil will come to our village; that Roman soldiers will come and do cruel things."

Artaban heard her timid speech and looked at the smiling child stretching rosy hands to him. His heart warmed.

Suddenly there was wild confusion in the streets. "The soldiers of Herod! They are killing our children!" came the wild cries.

The young woman's face grew white with terror. She clutched her child to her breast.

Artaban went to the doorway quickly. His broad shoulders filled the space from side to side.

The soldiers hesitated with surprise at the manner and dress of the stranger. The captain moved as if to thrust him aside. Artaban did not stir. His face was calm, and in his eyes there was a steady radiance.

In a low voice he said to the soldier, "I am all alone in this place, and I give this jewel to the prudent captain who will leave me in peace." He showed the ruby, glistening like a great drop of blood.

The captain gazed in amazement. Desire, greed were in his eyes and the lines of his face. He took the ruby and cried to his men: "March on! The house is empty."

Artaban returned to the cottage. "God of truth, forgive my sin, for I have lied. And two of my gifts are gone. I have spent for man that which was meant for my God and King."

But the young woman wept for joy and said gently, "You have saved the life of my little one! May the Lord bless you and keep you; the Lord make his face to shine upon you and be gracious to you; the Lord lift up his

countenance upon you and give you peace."

Artaban's search for the King was not at an end. Year followed year swiftly as he sought him now here and now there. He was seen in populous Egypt, seeking traces of the family who had fled from Bethlehem. At the foot of the pyramids, before the crouching Sphinx, in ancient Alexandria—to all these places and more he came.

A venerable Hebrew rabbi told him, "The King you seek will not be found in a palace, nor among the rich and powerful. The world is waiting for a new light, and a new kingdom to be established forever. I do not know how this shall come to pass. But this I know: Those who seek him will do well to look among the poor and the lowly, the sorrowful and the oppressed."

So the other Wise Man was seen again and again, searching among the scattered Hebrews where the family from Bethlehem might have found a place. He went to plague-stricken cities, the oppressed and afflicted in prison, the wretches in slave markets and on galley ships. In all these places of wretchedness he found none to worship, but many to help. He fed the hungry, clothed the naked, healed the sick, comforted the captive. And his years passed more swiftly.

Had he forgotten his quest? So it seemed. But now and again he took the pearl from a secret hiding place and looked at it in all its beauty. It grew more precious to him; his purpose for it was not dimmed, but heightened.

Thirty-three years of Artaban's life had passed, and he was still a pilgrim and a seeker. His hair was white, his eyes dull but smoldering.

Worn, weary, ready to die, he came again to Jerusalem as he had many times before. It was the season of the Passover; the city was thronged with strangers. But a singular agitation was on the multitude; a portentous gloom veiled the sky; a secret tide swept the crowd all one way.

Seeing a crowd of Parthian Jews, he asked the cause of the tumult. "We are going to Golgotha, to an execution," they said. "Haven't you heard? Two famous robbers and Jesus of Nazareth, who has done many wonderful works and is greatly loved by the people, are to be crucified."

The tired heart of Artaban beat unsteadily. Could this be the King whom he had sought for a lifetime? "Maybe I shall find my King at last, and shall come in time to offer my pearl for his ransom before he dies."

The old man followed the multitude with slow and painful steps. Just beyond the guardhouse a troop of soldiers came dragging a young girl with torn dress and disheveled hair. Seeing him she broke from her tormentors and threw herself at his feet. She had seen his white cap and the winged circle on his breast.

"Have pity on me," she cried, "and save me, for the sake of the God of Purity. I also am of the religion taught by the Magi. My father was a merchant of Parthia, but he is dead and I am to be sold as a slave for his debts. Save me from worse than death."

Artaban trembled. The old conflict in his soul was renewed, the conflict between the expectation of faith and the impulse of love.

Was this his great opportunity or his last temptation? But what he must do was inevitable, and does not the inevitable come from God? He was sure that he must do the true deed of love, to rescue this helpless girl.

He took the pearl from its hiding place and placed it in the slave's hand. "This is thy ransom, daughter! It is the last of my treasures which I kept for the King."

The darkness deepened; the earth trembled; houses rocked; stones crashed into the street. Artaban and the girl crouched helpless beneath the wall of the Praetorium.

The quest had failed, but there was peace. All was well because he had done the best that he could from day to day. He had been true to the light given to him.

The earth quivered again; a heavy tile struck the old man on the temple. He lay breathless and pale. The girl bent over him and saw that he was dying. She heard a voice, but saw no one. The old man's lips began to move, and she heard him say in the Parthian tongue:

"Not so, my Lord! For when saw I you hungry, or thirsty, or a stranger, or naked, or sick, and in prison? Thirty-three years have I looked for you; but I have never seen your face, nor ministered to you, my King."

He ceased, but the voice, sweet and faint, came again, and the girl heard: "Verily I say to you, inasmuch as you have done it unto one of the least of these my brethren, you have done it unto me."

Calm radiance and joy lighted the face of Artaban. His journey was ended. His treasures were accepted. The other Wise Man had found his King.

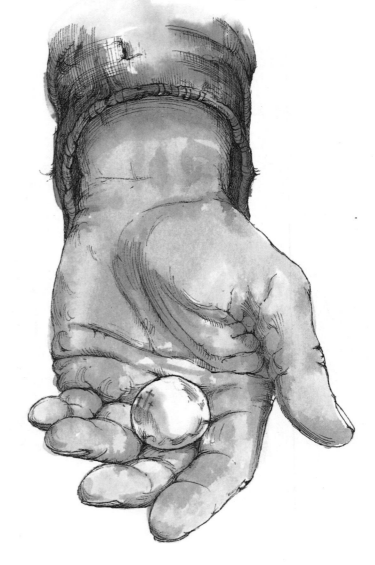

Anabasis of the Magi

ANDREW FIELD

Nous n'abiterons pas toujours ces terres jaunes.
(Saint-Jean Perse. l'Anabase.)

Camel bells ring out in the deep night
 as the caravan sweeps before the grim old
  mountain fortress—

The huge monolith rears up above us
 like a mythological beast from the fabled city of Ur,
its ridges pulled back like stony wings,
 covered with dry brush ready for the campfires;

The moon rides sleek above its back,
 through crosstrees made by precarious limbs
  that cling to a few inhospitable flecks of earth,
roots clawing down the flanks of the beast
 to find purchase—

We stop for the night's rest,
 and the tent, with its lamb's wool interior,
  sprawls in the blue-grey hush of light from above,
the moon like the flame of the Alexandrine pharos
 above our grateful gaze—

We unroll the parchment once again
 and by the fitful light of the lantern plot our course
  and scan the heavens for the sign of the star
   communion that has lured us westward.

In the morning we awaken
 to find snow choking the tent flap
  and blocking the smoke hole,
the fire gone quite out from the whip of the winds
 that have arisen in the great mountain fastness
  to the North:

Kings and camel drivers huddle together in the rugs,
 their geometric blue, red, and brown patternings
  soft reminders of the warm kingdoms
   by the side of the tropic sea,
 where the palms stand
  year-round sentinels robed in green.

Doubt invades us suddenly:
 two years out
  and no sign of the end of our travels—

But the image of the sun,
 the eye of God,
  revives our spirits and on we plunge,
a magi caravan moving on
 through the winter
  to the spring of Bethlehem.

Christmas Sojourn in San Diego

MARY C. NIXON

San Diego, California's southernmost city, sits in a landscape similar to Israel, the ancient birthplace of Jesus. To the east it is swaddled within a curve of golden, rock-strewn hills; to the west it is nourished by the tides of a white-capped sea. Although halfway around the globe from its Mediterranean counterpart, San Diego experiences a similar temperate climate and shares a vegetation rich in semitropical trees and flowering shrubs.

Sojourners from other parts of the country are bewildered at Christmas. They look about at the stark hills; they watch the heat of Santa Ana winds dry up the Christmas evergreens; they wander through exotic shopping centers, where customers are clad in shorts and sandals, and they cry out: How can this be Christmas? Nothing is traditional. Nothing is the way we remember from home. Can Christmas come to such a strange and alien place?

Yet Christmas does come. It strings itself along myriad canyons covered with masses of red-berried pyricantha bushes; it bursts forth in parks and gardens with the ubiquitous, bright poinsettias; it blooms and flowers across the tabletop mesas, brimming with red azaelia, pink fuchsia, and orange Bird of Paradise. It comes on the soaring wing of rust-colored hawks gliding over the canyons and in the persistent push of heavy fog creeping along the bays.

On a broad mesa overgrown with post-war homes, the first candle of Advent burns in Clairemont Lutheran Church, where the contemporary lines of a simple altar and pulpit are dressed in a rich, luminescent blue of hope. The Advent banner an-

Photo: San Diego harbor at Christmas.

nounces the season of preparation; soon the aisles and nave are flooded with adult and children's choirs singing contemporary Advent music. The worshipers come to attention, sit tall in the pews; something is expected, something is coming. The season is at hand.

The gifts of community during the first week of Advent are those to taste and see, to touch and smell. With the imaginative and exciting Horton Plaza in the revitalized downtown area acting as the hub, the shopping malls of San Diego become gala windows: each one a giant showcase strung with rows of colored lights, and tied up with bows of crinkling red and green.

Despite the urge to buy, consumerism is not king. One mall displays trees decorated by first-grade students: paper chains and representations of baby Jesus abound. Another mall auctions unique ornaments donated by local celebrities, the proceeds to be used for charity. In every center high-school bands and church choirs fill the air with carols. A local Baptist church enlightens the marketplace with a 12-foot-high "living Christmas tree." The smiles and voices of 40 choir members shine from fir and pine bough, proclaiming the message of salvation while shoppers stop to listen on their way from store to store.

Meanwhile, in Balboa Park near the heart of the city, a treat awaits the sojourner who celebrates "Christmas on the Prado"—a broad promenade of arches, columns, and lily ponds bordered by exotic flowers and shrubs. Spanish-Colonial museums and art galleries, built as temporary structures for the 1915-16 Panama-California Exposition, have been restored to their opulent ornamentation and historic old-world charm.

On December evenings, each museum and gallery is decorated in its Christmas finery. Each hosts an open house for the hundreds of families who burst upon the Prado with the same effervescence as the strings of colored lights frolicking and flirting along the walkways.

Every museum holds a surprise. High school bands, church bell ringers, or local Christmas carolers serenade in front of ancient dinosaurs or paintings by Renoir. Various clubs provide a variety of ethnic foods: chi-

li, krautdogs, pizza, hot cider, or sizzling nachos. Inside the Reuben H. Fleet Space Theater the Star of Bethlehem is projected across the 76-foot hemispherical dome.

The botanical clubs exhibit a dazzling display of seasonal decor using homegrown plants and winter flowers. The San Diego Historical Society hosts a wonderland of charming Christmas vignettes, which include treasures from some of the city's pioneer families, such as collections of dolls and trains, as well as exquisite table settings and designer trees.

A highlight of museum fare is found under the heavily ornamented belltower of the California Building. In its Museum of Man tables of Swedish handcrafts—along with meatballs, glogg, rosettes, and marzipan—are exhibited in front of the eerie, but fascinating, display of mummies and prehistoric man. In the midst of crowded merriment, the lights suddenly dim and a Santa Lucia procession begins, led by blond youths carrying gold stars aloft, white-robed maidens holding candles, and finally Saint Lucia wearing a crown of glowing candles atop her long golden hair. Swedish carols by the glow of candlelight remind the sojourner of a circle of lands around the globe and speak for a moment of a world that longs to be united in peace.

An evening at the park is climaxed with another candlelight procession, this one outside and led by several high-spirited school choirs and joined by a throng of spectators, many of whom are children carrying their own candles stuffed into soda bottles or other makeshift holders. The parade stops to admire a sparkling living Christmas tree and culminates in the outdoor organ pavilion, which twinkles with hundreds of gold lights like a magical castle in a mystical land.

San Diego claims the largest outdoor pipe organ in the world, donated in 1915 by John and Adolph Spreckels of Spreckels Sugar fame. Concerts have been given in the 2000-seat amphitheater every Sunday except during World War II. With tall palms swaying across the full moon, an old-fashioned carolsing is led by the dynamic sounds of

Photos: Preschool children decorating tree on Ocean Beach; outdoor organ pavillion; Horton Plaza.

the organ and the enthusiastic voices of high school students.

When candles finally burn to a sputter, families turn toward home. But first they make one final stop. In a line along the rear curve of the amphitheater, six houses host realistic life-sized, hand-carved nativity vignettes. With the gospel printed in both Spanish and English, the story unfolds: An angel announces the good news to Mary; a journey begins; a baby is born in a stable; the baby grows into a boy who faces the elders in the temple; finally, Jesus, now a man, blesses the children.

Sojourners and natives alike feel the blessing for themselves as they leave the park.

Not many years ago the wide valley that lines the San Diego River from the hills in the east to the Pacific in the west was simple pastureland for a few scattered farms. Today, Mission Valley has become a second heart of San Diego. It pulses with activity, moves the city's lifeblood along its intersecting freeways.

Against the sharp incline of the valley wall, the second candle of Advent glimmers within the stunning, inverted-U-shaped sanctuary of First United Methodist Church. Amid the bustle of the valley, an encounter with God is found in the generous gift of Bach's *Christmas Oratorio*, in which the congregation participates as well, lifting its voice to join the choir, orchestra, and organ for each of the 13 magnificent chorales.

In this second week of Advent, priceless gifts are given, to be savored and unwrapped slowly, collector's items for the house of memories. The sojourner can experience only a few.

A Christmas Carol, an original adaptation of Dicken's classic tale by Douglas Jacobs, is presented annually by the San Diego Repertory Theater. The audience is greeted by mimes and minstrels, then feasted on cookies and hot cider while awaiting the predictably late arrival of Mr. Dickens himself, who will read a new story this night.

A Festival of Christmas, a new and exciting Christmas musical for the entire family, is presented each year by the Lamb's Players Theater, an

intimate theater dedicated to superb drama with a Christian perspective. It is always a seasonal highlight.

In *The Nutcracker*, the Sugarplum Fairy, toy soldiers, and Mother BonBon come to life in this delightful ballet. Children and adults alike tuck away the memory to treasure.

Carols by Candlelight, an annual program presented by the First Assembly of God church, features the Christmas story and music in an 1850 New England village. The production involves a 60-voice choir and 40-piece orchestra.

A Festival of Lessons and Carols is presented by the University of San Diego in its Founder's Chapel, which is exquisitely decorated with red poinsettias and banks of white candles against a floor-to-ceiling gold altar. The festival awakens the soul to the joy of great music expertly sung. Yet the choir is only one example of hundreds of choral offerings. Indeed, during the Christmas season, all of San Diego bursts forth in a panoply of yuletide song. Hundreds of churches and schools share God's love in music.

The *Messiah*, both as concerts and sing-alongs, cannot be ignored. "I Handel'd the Messiah" T-shirts go on sale at the Civic Auditorium when thousands lift their voices with the Master Choral to sing this great work.

La Jolla is a Spanish phrase meaning "the jewel," a fitting name for this community of opulence by the sea. In 1982, the town council, tired of plastic Christmas decor, asked the local churches to create large banners on a background of purple. Thus the message is proclaimed all along the boulevards, above the boutiques and brokerage firms. Banners display the words HOPE and UNTO US—JESUS or a gold star leading Wise Men or a brilliant red cross above a manger. Here the wanderer discovers a white stucco church with a red-tiled Spanish roof, St. James by the Sea Episcopal, where the third Advent candle glimmers while the La Jolla University Civic Symphony and Chorus shares its own wondrous *Messiah* sing-along.

During this season when special care is traditionally given to animals, it is fitting that the city's largest "tree" radiates from the 320-foot tower at Sea World.

On a trip to Sea World children

Photos: Candlelight procession through mission courtyard; interior of Mission Basilica San Diego de Alcala; Balboa Park tree.

take along their warm jackets and mittens, despite temperatures in the 70s. For between the walruses and the dolphins, 900 tons of manmade snow have been piled on a 20-foot slope. A winter wonderland exists. For most San Diego children this will be their only chance to sled down a hill, build a snowman, throw a snowball, or simply squash the cold white stuff in their faces.

White is the color of snow, but red is the color of thousands of homegrown southland poinsettias. A short journey north to the Paul Ecke Poinsettia Ranch in Encinitas provides a feast in flower land. Used in homes and churches this plant is elegant; but blooming in vast red fields near the blue sea, it becomes a daytime spectacular.

Nighttime presents other gifts to San Diego. Gala boat parades can be seen from the grassy shores of Mission Bay or along the Embarcadero of San Diego Bay.

Led by the harbor patrol fireboat shooting arcs of water into the sky, little dinghies and large company-owned yachts form a flotilla of lights. Symbolic of the season, this parade intertwines the sacred and the secular like the holly and the ivy. Christmas trees made by stringing lights from the highest mast are most plentiful, but other vessels are lighted imaginatively. Various Santas sing out to the folks on shore from artificial chimneys, airplanes, or holly wreaths.

Those sailors who would present a religious theme create Bethlehem stars on their crafts and dress their families as characters of the nativity scene. A brass ensemble garbed like angels plays carols from one festive boat. A final dramatic ship glides in dark silence, the entire village of Bethlehem shrouded under its hidden lights while Wise Men are guided by a single bright star. And as the flotilla of lights finally passes from view, the spectators feel the spirit of community, a sense of family togetherness.

Whenever families venture out at night, the evening is not complete without a drive about the city to see the displays of lights. Built on a series of canyons and hills, San Diego provides hundreds of panoramas, all twinkling with color. Likewise, ships in the harbor—the ancient three-masted Star of India, the tuna fleet

with its towering riggings, even great destroyers and aircraft carriers owned by the navy—string lights to entertain the eye and heart.

A final surprise for the sojourner this week is found on a crisp, clear Wednesday evening where the city began, in Old Town during its Festival de la Posada. Early Spanish explorers discovered San Diego Bay in 1542, but not until 1769 did Spain set up its first tiny community along the bay's northeastern curve. Many of the original adobe *casas* have been preserved and restored. In addition, Spanish-style bazaars and restaurants add their own spicy flavors.

Before the festival begins, a walk through one such cluster, the Bazaar del Mundo, creates excitement. This charming courtyard blooms year round with hibiscus of every color. Small lighted trees add enchantment, while unique shops blaze with Mexican Christmas decor.

Tonight visitors find Old Town's winding lanes lined with 500 softly glowing *luminarias*, candles placed in brown paper bags and weighted with sand. Within this gentle glow and under the rustling leaves of the great eucalyptus and banana trees, *Las Posadas*—meaning "the lodgings"—reenacts Mary and Joseph's search for shelter in Bethlehem. The festival begins with an invocation and a reading of the Christmas story by Catholic priests and Protestant ministers. A créche is brought forth, carried aloft on a white and silver arc by men dressed in white with red sashes. Local school children portray the familiar characters: Mary, draped in blue robes, follows the arc astride a real donkey, accompanied by Joseph, the shepherds, the Wise Men, and a host of carolers all costumed in festive dress.

Around the square the procession moves, flanked by crowds of children riding on their father's shoulders, mothers pushing sleeping infants in strollers, and grade schoolers excited to carry their own lighted candles, everyone singing carols and stopping at the doors of the many historic buildings. At each stop Joseph sings (in Spanish) a haunting plea for lodging, and the innkeeper chants his refusal, even threatening to beat the poor couple if they do not go away.

Photos: Sombrero-clad Salvation Army bellringer; warm weather in mid-December; Santa piñata.

Past the Casa de Estudillo—with its four-foot thick adobe walls—around the cactus in front of San Diego's first frame building, the Newspaper Museum, under the loft of the old Seeley Stables the procession wanders, knocks, and implores. But always shelter is refused.

At long last one innkeeper capitulates. Shelter is found. Mary is helped from the donkey and the couple enter a warm adobe building amid cheers and applause by the crowd. A little child is heard to sigh and whisper the relief everyone feels: "Finally." More carols and the traditional breaking of a pinata stuffed with candy for the children polish off the night.

San Diego was first of all and will, perhaps, always be a mission. The sojourner is not here long before he or she feels the kindly presence of Father Serra, the Franciscan priest who founded California's first church in San Diego. And now, 200 years later, the fourth candle of Advent glows on the altar of Mission Basilica San Diego de Alcala, a tall narrow building. The stone floor is worn and uneven; the white adobe walls are painted and clean; the high ceiling is lined with hand-painted beams; the heavy doors are hewn from rugged wood. On this last Sunday evening before Christmas the unheated building is cold, but the worshipers who come for the candlelight concert bring it warmth. Sitting on the hard wooden benches, the sojourner feels the struggle and pain the early settlers must have endured. Looking at the worn stone floor, one can almost sense the moccasined feet of silent Indians gliding by.

A 70-voice choir sings the Christmas message from a rear loft; handsomely carved statues of Mary and Joseph sit on the floor before the altar. A votive light burns for a campfire and a canvas teepee arches above their heads. They have no baby yet, but rather sit and wait before their fire, wait among candles and fresh blossoming poinsettias for a baby to appear. Next to them stands a tree decorated with ornaments made by a choir member, each one hollowed out, lit from within, and containing an exact hand-carved miniature of an historic scene from the mission.

Photos: Boat parade; Las Posadas procession; Joseph and Mary in Las Posadas.

It is this great sense of mission that the wanderer discovers in San Diego during the final week before Christmas, when for the moment the homeless, the poor, the sick, and the lonely are sought out and brought into the fold; they are sheltered, fed, and clothed.

Sailors and marines, many of whom are away from home for the first time, are not forgotten either. The USO hosts hundreds of servicemen to dinners downtown and in private homes. And for those young men and women who prefer to remain on ship—feeling the closeness of their fellow sailors as extended family—a tree is erected in the cold steel mess, carols are sung, and a marathon meal befitting the finest hotel is served.

Across the border from San Diego lies Tijuana, a city rich in progress yet still housing pockets of dire poverty. Hundreds of children are abandoned each year, left to grow up in orphanages that can only provide them with the barest necessities. It is for American friends across the border, who share all year but especially at Christmas, to bring needed gifts—cuddly dolls and sturdy Tonka trucks, along with food, warm clothes, and large quantities of medicines and vitamins donated by businesses and families alike. Most important are the hugs and smiles from kind Americans who may not say "Feliz Navidad" with the right accent, but with a love the children cherish.

And thus the sojourner comes to the end of the journey. Christmas Eve arrives. In the old mission, under the flowing leaves of banana and palm trees, ghosts of Christmases past whisper to the new sojourners: We are all God's children, one family within our small world to protect and serve. Suddenly, under a sky full of star-shining hosts, a miracle occurs. Baby Jesus appears inside the teepee with Mary and Joseph. The campfire candle burns a little brighter, both on the hearth and in the heart.

"For unto us a child is born
Unto us a son is given."

It is Christmas, and San Diego is united in a spirit of God's overwhelming love. The tired and weary have discovered there is room in the inn.

The sojourner is home. Finally.

A COUNTRY SCHOOL CHRISTMAS

AS REMEMBERED
BY

Bob Artley

J ust as our one-room country school stood out on the lonely landscape, so did the Christmas season stand out in a rather monotonous school year.

School started each day at nine o'clock, and we had to run like crazy to get there before the bell stopped ringing.

Opening exercises usually consisted of the pledge of allegiance and the Lord's Prayer. Sometimes teacher read a chapter or two aloud from The Wizard of Oz, Black Beauty, or another of our favorite books.

After opening exercises, school started in earnest, some students reciting and the rest of us studying our lessons for our turn at recitation.

Along about mid-morning, just when it seemed we couldn't sit still another minute, we had recess. We all got bundled up in our coats, caps, scarves, boots, and mittens and had the time of our lives playing in the snow.

But just when we got well into our play the bell would ring and we would have to go back inside, get out of our coats, caps, scarves, boots, and mittens and take to learning again until noon. Then we would eat our packed lunches and get in some more play before the bell rang again.

For the older ones, the long periods of study and recitation were occasionally broken up by permission to go for coal or water.

After lunchtime there was more study and recitation, then afternoon recess, then learning again until it was time to go home, when we went "a hootin' an' hollerin'" out the door and down the road toward home.

BOB ARTLEY

Home from school meant grabbing a snack from the cookie jar, changing clothes, and going out to do chores.

After milking was done we washed up for supper, our favorite time, when the family was together sharing good food and the experiences of the day.

The evening was spent around the kerosene lamp doing homework, and reading or playing until bedtime.

"Time to get up!" came when it was barely light in order to give us plenty of time to do our morning chores, get cleaned up, eat breakfast, and walk the two miles to school without being tardy.

This was pretty much our routine most of the school year. But as the Christmas season approached our existence changed.

Two or three weeks before Christmas our study time was cut short each day so we could prepare for that great season. We decorated our schoolroom, practiced our parts for the Christmas program, made gifts for our parents, and drew names of those for whom we would bring gifts.

A day or two before the Christmas program the box containing the gingham curtains was brought down from the attic in the belfry. After the supporting wire was put up and the curtains strung on it, partitioning off the stage area, the atmosphere of the whole room was changed, giving a greater realism (and urgency) to our rehearsals.

BOB ARTLEY '95

Even though Christmas Day was a week away, its magic transformed our little schoolhouse into a wondrous place. The night of the program lights from the kerosene wall lamps and borrowed gas lanterns beckoned to us through the windows as we approached in the bobsled loaded with our family, baskets of food, and presents.

It was strange to see the schoolyard crowded with cars and horses hitched to bobsleds. The schoolroom itself bore little resemblance to the one we knew so well. It was jammed with people—our parents, siblings, relatives, friends, and neighbors. They were crowded into seats too small for them, on folding chairs in the aisles and along the walls.

It seemed the program was over very soon, for all the time and effort that was put into practicing and preparation.

Some of us forgot our lines, of course, but our audience didn't seem to mind. In fact, judging by their laughter, they liked those parts best. For the finale, the teacher had everyone join in singing "Joy to the World." This seemed to help put everyone in a joyful mood for the gift exchange and lunch that followed.

The exchange of gifts that followed was only for those of us in school, but the little ones in the audience each were given something too.

One thing these gatherings always did was bring out the very best from the kitchens of the neighborhood. Four or five different kinds of sandwiches, pies, cakes, cookies, and homemade candies came from the baskets and boxes that had been stacked in the corners until this point.

Finally, the food baskets, utensils and presents were gathered up, children were wrapped and buttoned against the cold ride home, good-byes and Merry Christmases were said, cars were cranked up, and horses were roused from their standing naps. Then we all headed for our homes, leaving the little schoolhouse to stand by itself on the dark, lonely prairie.

BOB ARTLEY '85

An Ancient Art Form

WILSON C. EGBERT

No story has so captured the imagination of poets and artists alike than the joyous appearance of an angel choir to humble shepherds and the quiet drama of a manger birth. The account of Jesus' birth, which appears in this volume, is illustrated in batik, a departure from the more familiar mediums of painting, sculpture, and photography.

For those of us so familiar with other art forms, batik may seem to us a second cousin, twice removed. Is it art? How is it done? Batik has been variously described as "wax writing," "wax drawing," or simply "writing and drawing." The word may come from the Javanese word *ambatik*, which is said to mean "cloth of little dots."

Batik is an artistic process whereby wax or another type of resist is applied to sections of a piece of fabric. The fabric is then exposed to dye, and only those parts of the fabric *not* coated with the resist accept the dye. The resist is then removed and applied to another segment of the fabric. This is then dyed with another color. This process is repeated for each color used. Careful planning is necessary so that the proper parts of the cloth are exposed to the dye at each step in the process. An understanding of color and how colors can be combined is also important as the fabric is exposed to a variety of dyes. In one sense batik is a reverse process. The artist applies the resist to all parts of the fabric *not* to be colored, eventually coloring the entire fabric.

Surveying history, it becomes plain that the dyeing of cloth was a widespread skill. In the Greek and Roman civilizations dyes had been widely used. The book of Acts speaks of Lydia, a seller of purple. Indigo plants furnished a blue dyestuff, and madder furnished a red dyestuff for many countries. Apparently other vegetative materials, plants and barks, were used by early dyers. But there seems to be no forerunner of the decorative batik style in the Mediterranean world—except, perhaps, in Egypt.

An ancient headdress made by a process related to batik has been found in Egypt. The method of dyeing, called *ikat kapala*, involved covering the yarn at different points and then using several dyes. Imagine the designing foresight and skills needed to weave such yarns into a pattern!

Although it is impossible to determine exactly when people began decorating fabric with batik, there is general agreement that this activity is at least 5000 years old.

Experts take sides on the place of origin for batik itself. Some say it originated in China, for weaving and tie dyeing were highly developed in the Táng Dynasty (618-906 A.D.). According to this theory, the art spread to India and Japan from China. There are examples of eighth century batik screens, probably by Chinese artists, preserved in Japan's Nara Museum.

Others surmise that batik originated in India. They point to the early excellence of Indian dyers to support their claim. It is thought that the famous indigo dye was developed early in India and then became available to the Javanese.

Whatever its origin, batik reached the height of its development in Java. Cambodia and Bali share the same batik process but not Java's reputation. A Javanese temple, built about 1200 A.D., shows statues garbed in carved versions of a batik design. Evidence suggests that batik came to Java much earlier.

Dutch control of Java and the formation of the Dutch East Indies Company brought batik to the Western world. Leaders of 17th century fashion scrambled for these Indonesian imports. The imports were apparently a success as batiks appeared all over Europe. Artists were moved to try batik. Merchants and printers tried to reproduce batiks by printing on cloth. Artists succeeded in simplify-

Batik artist Carol Martin consults a pencil sketch when applying color to cloth.

ing the process, but commercial reproduction would need to wait for 20th century technology. The post-World War II period also brought into being some 10,000 village factories in Java.

In the 1960s and 70s interest in batik stirred in the United States. Courses on batik art and craft began to appear in college catalogs. Batik was recognized as a significant art form.

Batik artists employ three elements in working their craft: fabric, dyes, and resist. For those three elements, artists select from several options, depending on the detail required and the use of the completed batik artwork.

Varicolored dyes are used on a variety of fabrics. The Javanese had available only a few dyes, such as indigo and brown from *soga* bark. The intense red dyes of cochineal and antimony may have become available to dyers worldwide only af-

A wax resist insures that only the desired areas of the cloth absorb the dye.

mon resist to dyes used in fine Javanese batiks. A rice paste was also developed for use when fine detail was not necessary.

Today wax resist is made from a mixture of paraffin and beeswax. Proportions vary according to the effect desired, usually three or four parts of paraffin to one part of beeswax. The more beeswax used, the sharper the line between dyed and undyed areas. Paraffin cracks more easily and makes possible the fine dye lines seen on batik pieces.

Flour or starch-based resists can also be used if the dye or pigment is brushed on. If the fabric is dipped into dye, however, wax resist must be used.

The tools for applying wax resist are Oriental bamboo brushes or the traditional Javanese *tjanting* (pronounced chän-ting). The brushes come in various sizes with tapered points to allow the laying down of fine or wide lines.

ter trade was established with the New World. But the real revolution in dye-making came with the introduction of aniline dyes in the 19th century. Today the batik artist or craft worker faces a wide assortment of color and dyes for special processes.

The cloth available to early batik makers was cotton or silk. This was prepared by repeated washings in hot water. A weak solution of soda or ashes of rice stalks was added to each washing. Between washings and dryings, the cloth was steeped in coconut or castor oil to open the fibers. After the final washing, the cloth was dried, lightly starched, loosely rolled, and beaten until it became pliable. Then the fabric was hung on a vertical frame to dry.

Contemporary batik creators have a different set of choices to make about cloth. Natural fibers are still the best choice, whether cotton or silk, wool or linen. The sizing in most fabrics can be washed out. More difficult is the need to rid fabrics of the compounds that may be used in some no-iron cloth. Most difficult to use are combinations of synthetic and natural fibers.

Silk seems to be the most desirable choice for fine articles of clothing or for screens and decorative purposes. Cotton and wool furnish sturdy materials for practical items, although wool does not do well for intricate designs.

The third ingredient in batik creation is the resist. The resist is applied to the fabric; at those places the dye will not color the fabric. Wax was apparently the most com-

Brushes can also be used to apply dye to large areas of a batik design.

The *tjanting* is a copper or bronze cup to which a spout or spouts (from one to four spouts) have been soldered. A wooden handle completes the instrument. The *tjanting* is dipped into hot wax; the wax is poured out carefully, making lines, circles, and dots on the cloth. It takes some practice to master this technique.

Batik is an exciting medium for artists. The design grows on the fabric as some areas are exposed to the dye and others are excluded; as colors mingle and collide, creating new hues; as drab, wet colors take on brilliance as they dry.

The Christmas story in this issue is a fine example of this medium. Take a moment to study the batik illustrations of Mary, the angels and the shepherds, the stable in Bethlehem, the three Wise Men, and the flight to Egypt. Note how the figures have been formed, how each part has been fashioned and joined to the rest of the figure. Notice how dyes have been mixed, one on top of another, to form new colors. Examine an expanse of color and see how it is, in fact, made up of a variety of tones. Note the fine lines in the fabric where the resist has cracked and dye has invaded. Marvel at the brilliant colors; marvel at the soft colors. Imagine how many times each piece of fabric was dipped into the dye vat.

Wonder at this ancient art form, begun so long before Jesus' birth. How beautifully it pictures the coming of the Savior.

Our Christmas

Christmas Eve _____
_____
_____
_____

Christmas Day _____
_____
_____
_____

Christmas Worship _____
_____
_____

Christmas Guests	Christmas Gifts
_____	_____
_____	_____
_____	_____
_____	_____
_____	_____
_____	_____
_____	_____

Christmas
Photo